LEARN TO DRAW
MANGA
A Step-by-Step Guide

EMMETT ELVIN

BARNES
&NOBLE
BOOKS
NEW YORK

This edition published by Barnes & Noble, Inc.,
by arrangement with Kandour Ltd UK

2004 Barnes & Noble Books

ISBN 0-7607-5096-3

M 10 9 8 7 6 5 4 3 2 1

All rights reserved. No part of this publication may be reproduced, stored in a
retrieval system, or transmitted, in any form or by any means, electronic,
mechanical, photocopying, recording or otherwise, without written permission in
accordance with the provisions of the Copyright Act 1956 (as amended). Any
person or persons who do any unauthorised act in relation to this publication
may be liable to criminal prosecution and civil claims for damages.

Kandour Ltd has made every effort to ensure that the content of this book was
accurate at the time of publication. The publisher, author and editors cannot be
held liable for any errors and omissions in this publication or actions that may be
taken as a consequence of using it.

Created by Metro Media Ltd, UK
Author and illustrator: Emmett Elvin
Managing editors: Emma Hayley, Jenny Ross
Cover and text design: Emmett Elvin
Page layout and design assistance: Eugene Felder

© Kandour Ltd

Printed in China

CONTENTS

FOREWORD

Learn to Draw Manga is an easy-to-follow, step-by-step guide to creating your own manga comic strips. Along the way, you will gain a solid understanding of all the main principles of drawing – from basic figure construction to perspective and beyond. This is for budding artists of all abilities and all ages. Even if you've never forayed into the world of manga, the book's simple step-by-step approach allows the complete novice to gain essential drawing skills. Equally, you may already be highly experienced in drawing your own manga universe, but your inking is letting you down or the hands you draw look like mangled frankfurters. Whatever your level, this book is designed to be a fun way to improve your drawing skills.

Over the years I've seen many 'how to' books. Some are very good, some are precious little use to anyone. In writing this book I have tried to address my reservations about them all. As a result, this volume covers every aspect of drawing for manga, but avoids unnecessary detail you will almost certainly never use. My aim has been to allow you to start creating your own manga in the fastest possible time.

I've also packed in some of the best secrets and tricks I've learned over the ten-plus years I've been doing this, most of which you won't have seen anywhere else.

Manga is the most exciting and vibrant form of comic art on the planet right now. There's no better time to gain the skills, either as a hobby or a pro.

Emmett Elvin
Author

ORIGINS

The Breaking Wave off Kanagawa, woodblock color print by Hokusai, from the series *Thirty-six Views of Mount Fuji*, 1826–33

In 1814, the legendary Japanese artist Hokusai used the term 'manga' to describe his woodcuts. Although Hokusai made manga his own, these kinds of picture stories had, in fact, been around in Japan for over 1,000 years. After Hokusai's huge influence on manga, the genre began to develop further by the end of the 19th century when Japanese interest in Western forms of culture and storytelling flourished. But we have to go to the 1940s to find the real birth of what we recognize as modern manga.

THE GOD OF MANGA

Although there are a few hugely important figures in Western comic history, such as Will Eisner and Jack Kirby, none of them can compare with the impact one lone figure has had on manga. Japanese animator Osama Tezuka is the undisputed god of manga. Why? Although Tezuka had a fondness for the illustrated stories of his time, he felt they lacked real substance, emotion and the ability to engage the reader. Being an avid fan of European movies, he strove to bring some of their depth and innovative presentation to his vision of what manga could be. With the 1947 debut of his book *New Treasure Island* he changed manga overnight, selling a staggering 400,000 copies.

Tezuku extended his vision of manga by creating anime, which has become the worldwide term for Japanese-style animation, be it for television, feature films, or videos. The West's first taste of Tezuka's vision was in 1961 with the broadcast of the TV show *Tetsuwan Atom* – better known as *Astro Boy* in the West. Because manga has such a close affiliation with its animated sibling anime, it's not surprising how close the two mediums are in appearance and approach.

The tradition began with *Astro Boy* and continued with shows such as *Battle of the Planets* in the '70s, and then in the '80s with *Bladerunner*-inspired *Akira*, the movie that probably did more than any other to bring anime to a truly international audience. The tradition continues still with titles such as Rumiko Takahashi's *Ranma 1/2* and Masamune Shirow's *Patlabor Mobile Police* and *Ghost in the Shell*.

Western comics have never enjoyed the same close relationship, although in recent years with the advent of *Batman The Animated Series*, and the *Superman* animated series we've seen a lot more cross-fertilization. This is largely due to artists such as Bruce Timm and Paul Dini who seem happy enough (not to mention talented enough) to work in both comic books and animation.

WHAT IS MANGA?

Maybe the question should be: "What makes manga so different from other comic art forms?" Look at these two images. They are both the same scene, but are rendered in two radically different ways:

1. Manga has never been that concerned with making characters look realistic. In the West however, if your comic book characters aren't realistic, you'll be called a 'cartoonist'!

2. Manga makes heavy use of gray tones to give the images depth. The West on the other hand has a decades-long tradition of full-color printing, letting a separate person, the colorist, take care of that side of things.

3. In manga there are lots of 'speed lines' or other special effects devices. For all its muscle-bound machismo, Western comics do not go quite so overboard.

4. Manga tends to be less dialogue-heavy, preferring to let the artwork convey character depth and emotion.

5. Backgrounds are often given far more attention in manga. Generally, they are more technical and architecturally accurate.

6. A lot of manga features characters with oversized eyes – but not all manga.

CHAPTER 1

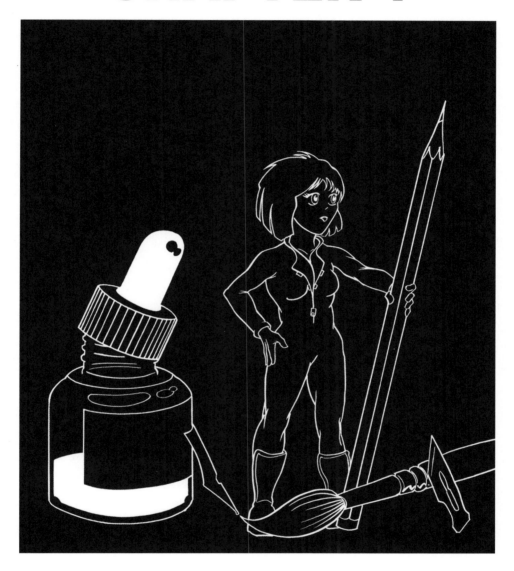

MATERIALS

MATERIALS

STUFF YOU MUST HAVE

1. Pencils. Duh! If you're not doing rough layouts with a blue pencil (see page 13) then do the breakdowns in a light graphite pencil (usually an H or 2H), using a darker (HB or B) for the final tight pencils (more of that in the next chapters).

2. A good eraser. The best is a putty eraser. Although they are more expensive, they are much better at picking up pencil marks. They can be kneaded into points for getting into tight spots and won't smudge your lines.

3. A craft knife. This is the best tool for getting a good, sharp point on your pencil. Working with a blunt pencil is like darning socks with a pool cue – fun, but ultimately useless. It's also good for lifting off that half-pint of whiteout you've just spilled on your artwork.

4. A good, hard-edged ruler. A cork-backed metal rule is great – because the edge doesn't make contact with the paper, it can be used for inking lines and borders.

5. Paper. You'll want some bleed proof paper (non-bleed proof will give you a fuzzy line when it comes to inking). A marker pad is fine, though generally a little thin. The best stuff for the job is Bristol paper – extremely smooth, heavyweight, bleed proof and the choice of most professionals.

6. Brushes and/or pens. You'll probably need to experiment with brushes, dip pens and markers before you find out what is best for you. I usually use a small (either 0 or 1 size) brush quite heavily loaded with ink. This gives a hard, even line but takes a bit of controlling. Some people hate brushes and only ever use pens – use whatever gets you the result you're looking for (more of this in chapter 11).

7. Some good quality Indian Ink. Indian Ink contains shellac, which makes it permanent. You should never ink with non-permanent ink – one spillage of water and you'll have an unsalvageable mess on your hands.

8. Process white. A highly opaque paint, great for putting white on black, as well as fixing inking mistakes.

OTHER STUFF YOU'LL FIND USEFUL

1. Flexible curve. Like a plastic bendy toy, the center of this tool is a length of wire. This allows you to flex it into a variety of arcs and s-shapes. Very handy to begin with but as your confidence in line drawing improves you'll find yourself using it less and less.

2. Blue pencil. This is the standard 'layout' pencil for animators and comic artists. The color is also referred to as 'non-repro blue' for the simple reason that it's invisible to photocopiers and other grayscale scanning equipment. So what? It means you don't have to erase it. It's also easier to see your 'tight' pencils over. Available at most good graphic supplies shops.

3. Set squares and elliptical curves. There's a whole array of geometric-type tools out there. Set squares are good for making sure your borders are exactly 90 degrees (at least when you want them to be). Ellipse templates can be handy for quickly drawing speech balloons.

4. Computer and scanner. If you don't have a computer there's no need to panic. They are mainly used at the end of the process for finishes and general readying for print. We'll have more of that in a much later chapter.

5. A light box. Not cheap to buy, but it is possible to make your own with some elementary carpentry and electrical skills – ensure you have professional supervision. It's essentially a wooden box with a strip-type light bulb inside. The top has a transparent panel and a switch for the light at the side (see right). This is an invaluable tool. Why?

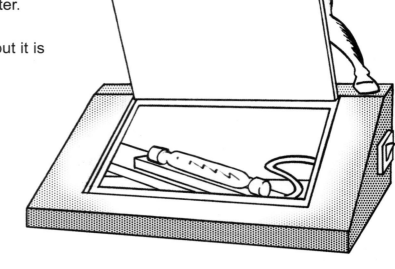

Suppose you are in the middle of a six-panel page but the fifth panel is just driving you nuts. No matter how many ways you try it, you just can't get Monster Girl's legs to look right at that angle. Now your panel is a horrible gray mess of 2,000 chewed-up and erased pencil lines.

The answer?

On a separate sheet of paper, use the light box to draw several panels the size of the one you're working on. Do it as many times as you like until you get it just how you want it. When you've got it right, place the now-brilliant panel on the light box and put the original page on top. Flip the light switch and trace your new drawing on to the page.

Hey presto – problem solved.

A good light box makes a fine general purpose drawing surface too – it's the standard drawing table of animation studios the world over.

That just about covers the materials.

We'll have a quick look at using pencils, and then we'll start drawing.

HOW TO HOLD A PENCIL

'What? Are you serious'?

I couldn't be more serious. How we hold a pencil has a massive impact on the kind of line we produce. Ultimately, the grip on our pencil is a personal matter and no two people draw exactly the same way. You'll arrive at the grip which is right for you. However, there are techniques which will definitely improve the expressive quality of our line.

Look at the two drawings below:

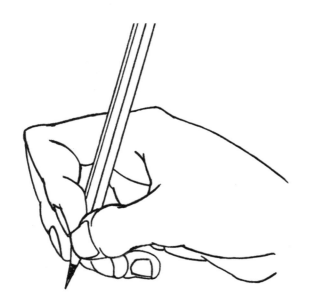

In the first drawing (left), the pencil is held too close to the tip. This allows the pencil far too much freedom to wobble as we draw. The result? A lack of control over the line.

In the second drawing (below), the pencil is held much higher up. This restricts its movement, eliminating 'line wobble' and giving greater control.

With the pencil held the second way, we can use the natural arc of our wrist to produce smooth, flowing lines and curves. For larger curves we can even use our elbow as a pivot to produce perfect, wobble free lines.

It may seem a little unnatural at first, but try it – you'll be glad you did.

CHAPTER 2

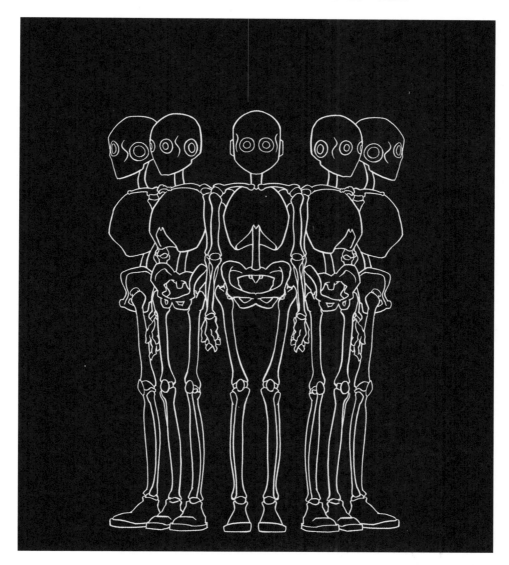

THE BARE BONES

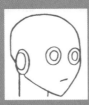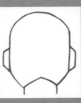

BASIC ANATOMY 1

THE ANDROID FACTORY

Skeletons are great. They provide us with the fundamentals of what we need to show a character in action. Animators often use nothing more than a 'wireframe' character, essentially a skeleton, to work out and illustrate postures and actions of their characters.

It's a very fast and effective method of working out the position and posture of our characters on the page when we draw manga, but first we have to learn the basics.

It's not the aim of this book to give you page after page of extreme anatomical detail. There are books, sometimes hundreds of pages long, that do that. And I thoroughly recommend getting your hands on one and taking the time to study it. The deeper our knowledge of anatomy, the better equipped we are to draw our characters in any way our imaginations desire.

What you need to get you started is a basic understanding of the major points of action of a skeleton. This means gaining an understanding of the major bones and joints and their relationship to one another.

At this point I'm going to hand you over to my assistant, Honegumi, an android at the Bioneering Corporation. She can show you very graphically what I mean…

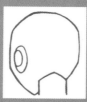

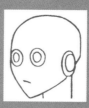

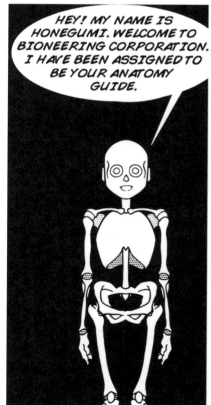

HEY! MY NAME IS HONEGUMI. WELCOME TO BIONEERING CORPORATION. I HAVE BEEN ASSIGNED TO BE YOUR ANATOMY GUIDE.

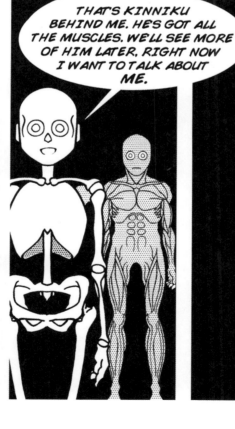

THAT'S KINNIKU BEHIND ME. HE'S GOT ALL THE MUSCLES. WE'LL SEE MORE OF HIM LATER, RIGHT NOW I WANT TO TALK ABOUT ME.

I'LL TAKE YOU TO THE SKELETON ROOM. WE CAN HAVE A GOOD LOOK AT WHAT MAKES A BODY WORK. DON'T BE SCARED – THEY'RE ONLY SYNTHETIC SKELETONS!

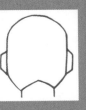

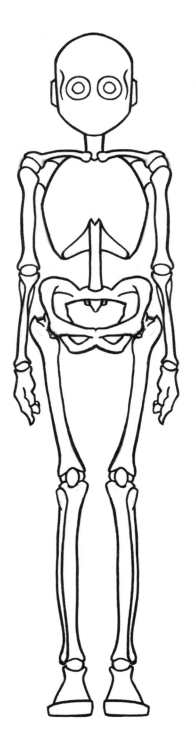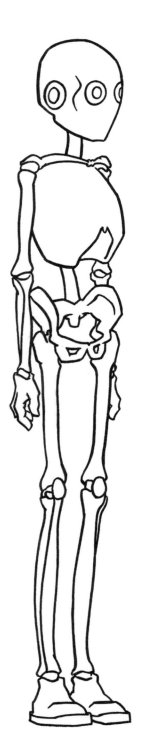

These pictures show the skeleton from a variety of viewpoints. Please notice that none of the bones are straight. They are all either curved or tapered.

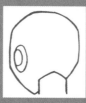

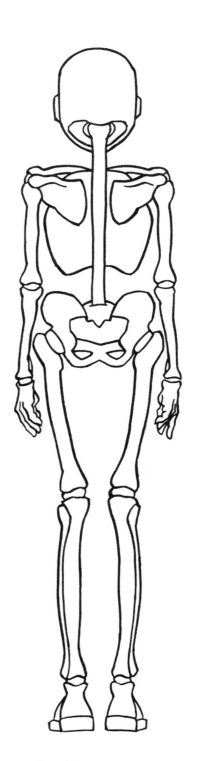

In anime, this series of pictures is known as a 'turnaround' or 'character rotation'. To be a good manga artist we must learn to draw the body from all angles.

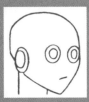
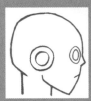

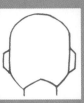

THE PELVIS

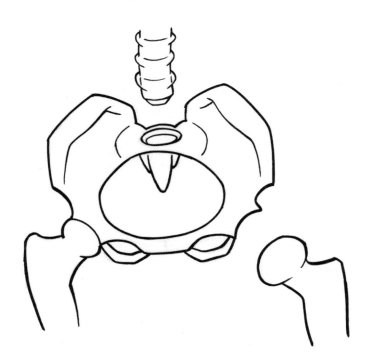

The pelvis is the 'hub' of the body. As shown on the left, it sits on top of the legs and supports the spine and as a result, every part of the upper body.

The pelvis can be extremely expressive too. It's the one thing you have to get right when drawing sexy poses.

This is a front view of the pelvis showing how the thighbone fits into it.

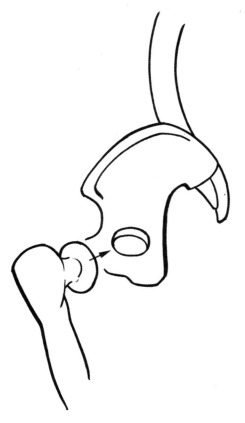

The thighbone sockets are located at roughly 4 and 8 o'clock on each side of the body.

The spine inserts into another socket located at the back and center of the pelvis. Continuing on from that point is what would be our tail – if we were further down the evolutionary scale.

Very roughly speaking, the pelvis is bowl-shaped, but with the front cut away. Its movement is only restricted by the relative positions of the thighbones and spine.

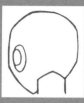

These rough pencil 'breakdowns' show the pelvis in action. It can thrust forwards or backwards, swing out to the left or right or gyrate. Experiment with drawing characters like the ones below.

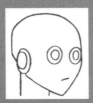
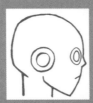

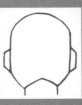

THE LEG BONES

FEMUR

This is the thighbone. It's the biggest one in the entire body and is at least one quarter of our entire body length.

The most noticeable thing apart from its size is the peculiar ball-like lump sticking out from the top. Why should it be shaped this way?

This is the part that fits into the pelvis and so needs to stay clear of the large pelvic bone. This allows for very good, unhindered movement.

TIBIA AND FIBULA

These two bones make up the lower leg. The big one you'll know as your shinbone, but you may not even be aware of its much smaller partner. It's attached at the top at the knee and forms your outer ankle. The rest of it is buried deep under your muscle, so it's a bit of a secret.

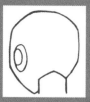

THE ARM BONES

HUMERUS

The upper arm bone looks a bit like a smaller version of the thighbone and similarly has a double knuckle joint at the bottom.

Where it differs from the thighbone is that the top attaches to the shoulder. The ball joint doesn't need to protrude as much either.

RADIUS AND ULNA

You're far more likely to be aware of the two bones in your forearm as they are both mostly near the surface. You should be able to distinguish between them by feeling your wrist.

The ulna is much thicker at the top and forms the bulk of the elbow. The radius on the other hand is thicker at the bottom, making up most of the wrist.

Because of the construction of the elbow, these bones twist and cross over forming an 'x' shape when we swivel our wrists.

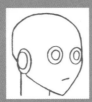

THE RIB CAGE AND SPINE

RIB CAGE

The rib cage and spine form the most complex area of the skeleton.

For our purposes we don't need to be too concerned with individual ribs as we will hardly ever need to draw them. However, a quick word about their structure and behavior will help our understanding of how they work.

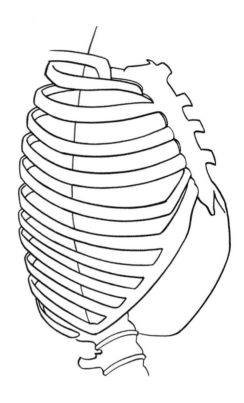

As we breathe in and out the rib cage actually stretches. Not the ribs themselves, but the areas of cartilage which join them to the bone at the front called the sternum.

THE SPINE

The spine runs down the back of the rib cage forming a shape like a stretched out 's'. It is made up of many small bones between which sits a rubbery tissue, because of this the spine is very flexible and can move to a greater or lesser extent in all directions.

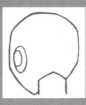

These rough pencil 'breakdowns' show the rib cage and spine in action. It can thrust forwards or backwards, swing out to the left or right or gyrate. Experiment with rib and spine drawings by using these simplified models.

MALE AND FEMALE SKELETONS

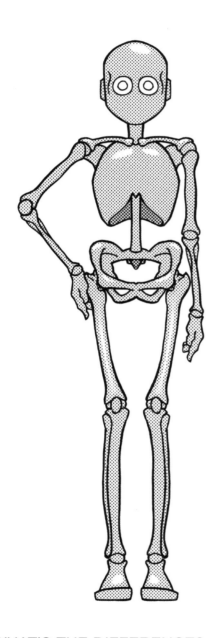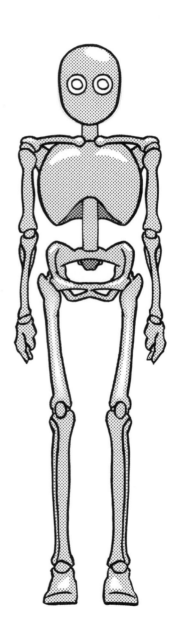

WHAT'S THE DIFFERENCE?

Compare this female android skeleton (left) with her male counterpart. His hips are narrower and his shoulders are wider, giving him a broader chest.

PROPORTION

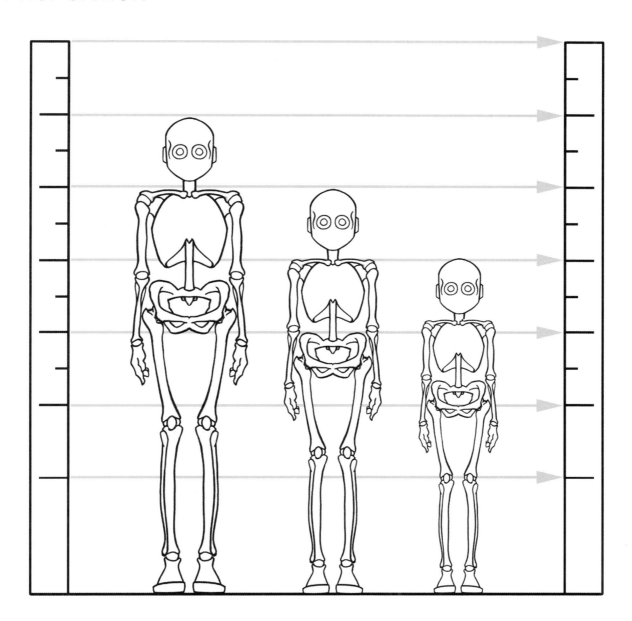

When we look at a character in manga, if they're at least semi-realistic, we have a good idea of their size. They may appear on their own, but we still know whether they're seven-footers or pint-sized.

How? The most important indicator of their size is the relation of head to body. Look at the chart above. No matter what height a person is, head size is always roughly the same for everyone.

LOCOMOTION

Drawing mini-skeletons in action is a great, fast way to try out various body positions. Try drawing them running, jumping, kicking, dancing, as shown above.

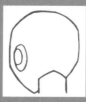
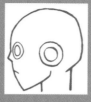
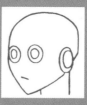

Now we've got all the information we need to draw the skeletal form, let's put the Honegumi skeleton through its paces:

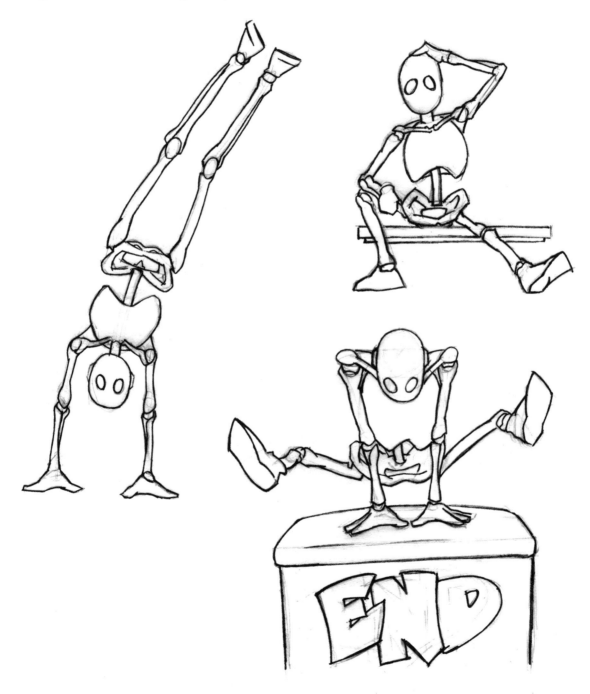

CHAPTER 3

MUSCLES

BASIC ANATOMY 2

PUTTING FLESH ON THE BONES

Because the skeleton is inflexible it is fairly simple to draw. It behaves in a predictable way, with each bone retaining its particular shape at all times.

Muscle, however, is a completely different matter. It stretches, squashes and bends, depending on the type of movement taking place. It's this change in the shape of the muscle that tells us what kind of action a character is engaged in.

This can present a lot of problems when starting out. But if we have a good understanding of how muscles work in relation to the skeleton it can go a long way to helping us get it right.

There are a few simple rules we can learn. If we stick to them, even the most complicated muscle groups will present no barrier to us. We'll be able to produce completely convincing characters every time.

Over to Honegumi again...

THIS IS KINNIKU – THE NEXT LEVEL OF ANDROID HERE AT BIONEERING. AS YOU CAN SEE, KINNIKU IS FLESH COVERED.

SYNTHETIC LIGAMENTS JOIN HIS MUSCLES TO HIS BONES.

EXCUSE ME, KINNIKU – I'M GOING TO DISASSEMBLE YOU TO SHOW THE READERS HOW YOU WORK.

EXCELLENT.

THIS, AS YOU CAN SEE IS KINNIKU'S ARM. IT'S CONSTRUCTED JUST THE SAME WAY AS YOUR OWN ARM – JUST A LITTLE SIMPLER. THERE'S NO SKIN ON THIS ARM YET.

THIS LETS US SEE THE MUSCLE CONSTRUCTION MORE EASILY.

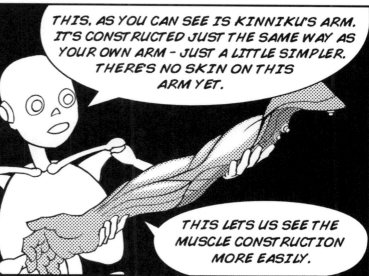

COULD YOU FLEX YOUR ARM MUSCLES, PLEASE KINNIKU?

THANKS.

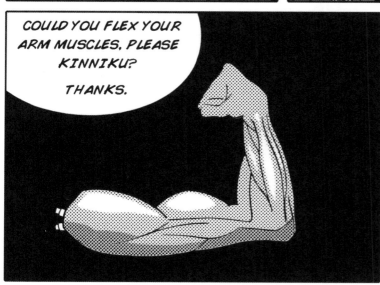

AS YOU CAN SEE, WHEN THE ARM MUSCLES FLEX, THEY HARDEN AND PRODUCE A MORE PRONOUNCED SHAPE.

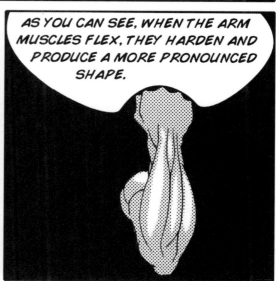

THE MOST NOTICEABLE CHANGE IS IN THE BICEP, THE BIGGEST MUSCLE IN THE ARM. LET'S FLIP IT OVER AND LOOK AT THE BACK OF THE ARM.

SEE HOW THESE MUSCLES ALL JOIN AT THE ELBOW? FLEX PLEASE, KINNIKU!

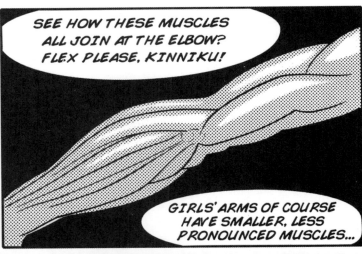

GIRLS' ARMS OF COURSE HAVE SMALLER, LESS PRONOUNCED MUSCLES...

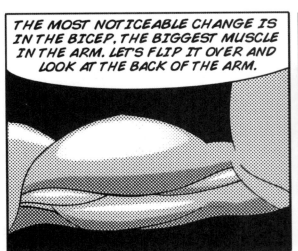

MALE   FEMALE

...THOUGH THEIR CONSTRUCTION IS ESSENTIALLY THE SAME. HERE'S A PICTURE COMPARING THEM.

NOW LET'S HAVE A LOOK AT KINNIKU'S TORSO. **Wow!** THERE'S A LOT OF MUSCLES TO TALK ABOUT HERE!

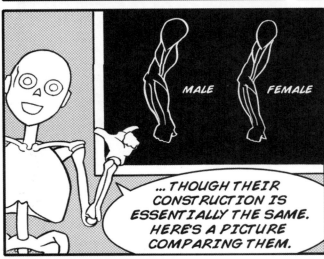

THE BIGGEST MUSCLES ON THE TORSO ARE THESE LARGE CHEST MUSCLES CALLED PECTORALS, OR 'PECS'.

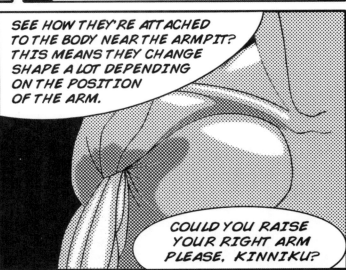

SEE HOW THEY'RE ATTACHED TO THE BODY NEAR THE ARMPIT? THIS MEANS THEY CHANGE SHAPE A LOT DEPENDING ON THE POSITION OF THE ARM.

COULD YOU RAISE YOUR RIGHT ARM PLEASE, KINNIKU?

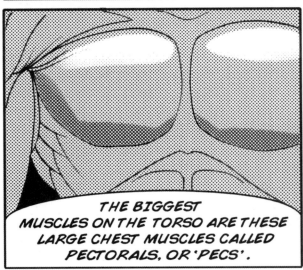

WITH THE ARM RAISED, THE MUSCLE STRETCHES AND FLATTENS, COVERING A LARGER AREA.

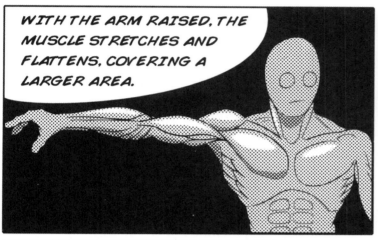

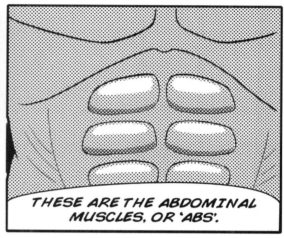

THESE ARE THE ABDOMINAL MUSCLES, OR 'ABS'.

BECAUSE THERE'S NO BONE UNDERNEATH THEM THEY'RE EXTREMELY FLEXIBLE.

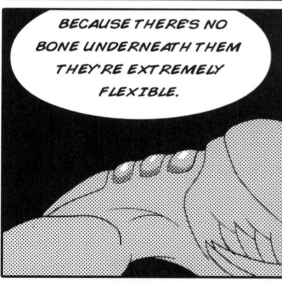

THERE ARE THREE MAIN 'PAIRS' OF ABS AND A FOURTH, FLATTER PAIR THAT RUNS DOWN TOWARDS THE GROIN.

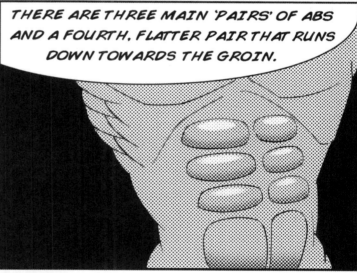

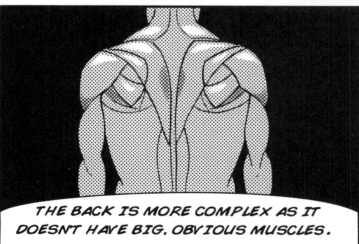

THE BACK IS MORE COMPLEX AS IT DOESN'T HAVE BIG, OBVIOUS MUSCLES.

WHEN THE BACK ARCHES, THESE MUSCLES ABOVE THE BUTTOCKS STICK OUT. OOH!

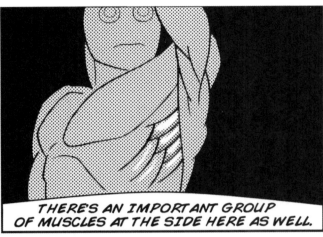

THERE'S AN IMPORTANT GROUP OF MUSCLES AT THE SIDE HERE AS WELL.

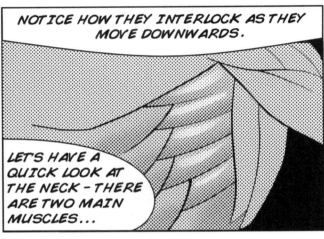

NOTICE HOW THEY INTERLOCK AS THEY MOVE DOWNWARDS.

LET'S HAVE A QUICK LOOK AT THE NECK – THERE ARE TWO MAIN MUSCLES...

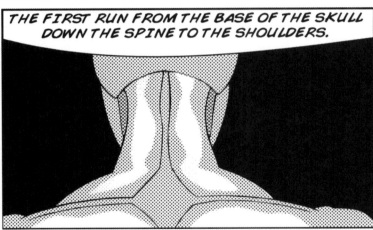

THE FIRST RUN FROM THE BASE OF THE SKULL DOWN THE SPINE TO THE SHOULDERS.

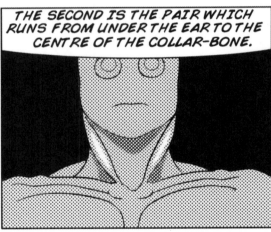

THE SECOND IS THE PAIR WHICH RUNS FROM UNDER THE EAR TO THE CENTRE OF THE COLLAR-BONE.

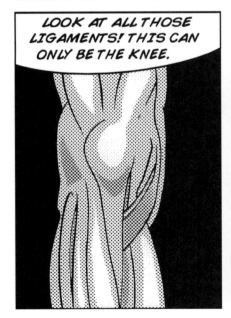

LOOK AT ALL THOSE LIGAMENTS! THIS CAN ONLY BE THE KNEE.

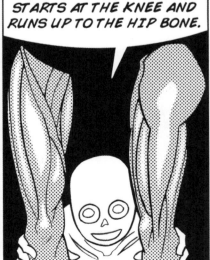

ON THE UPPER LEG, THE BIG MUSCLE AT THE FRONT STARTS AT THE KNEE AND RUNS UP TO THE HIP BONE.

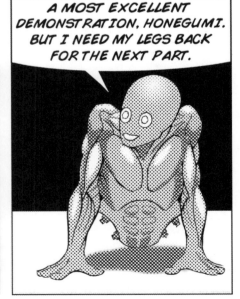

A MOST EXCELLENT DEMONSTRATION, HONEGUMI. BUT I NEED MY LEGS BACK FOR THE NEXT PART.

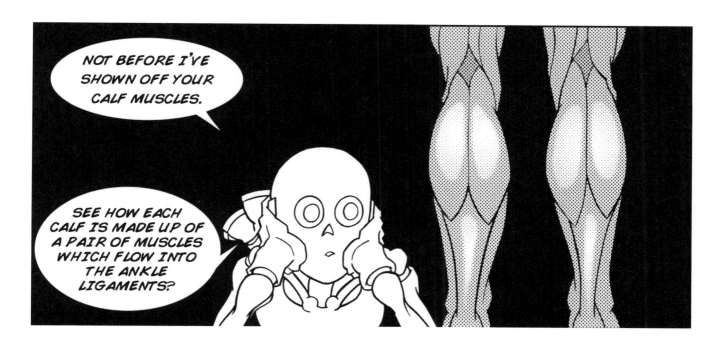

Above is a typical muscle. Narrow and tough at the ends and wide and squidgy at the center. If you know where the ligaments start and end, the muscles you draw will always be in the right place.

THE FEMALE BODY

The muscles on the female body differ very little from the male.

With the exception of the buttocks and breasts they tend to be smaller or less pronounced.

The illustrations here show the kind of female body found only on top athletes. On the female form there tends to be more fatty tissue covering the muscle fibres, resulting in an ultimately smoother, more rounded form.

The breasts are the most obvious departure from the male. These vary in size and shape, though as a guideline the bosom in manga is usually more realistically proportioned than in Western comics.

The increased size of the hips results in fuller buttocks and the thighs are wider at this point.

The waist should be narrower than for males and remember to make the feet and hands slightly smaller on females.

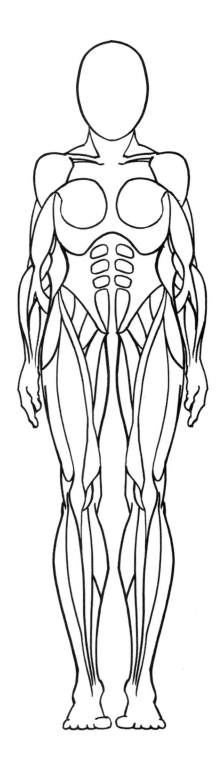

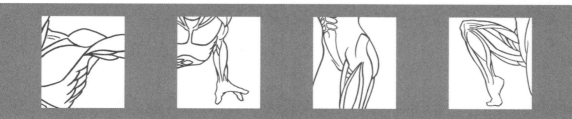

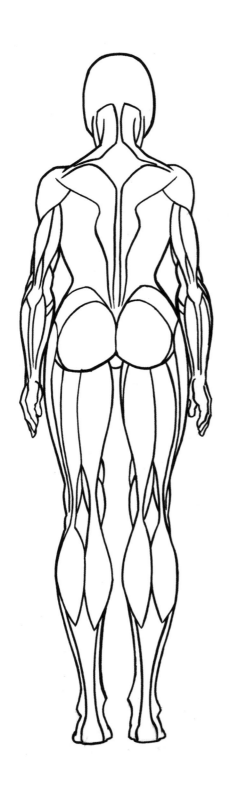

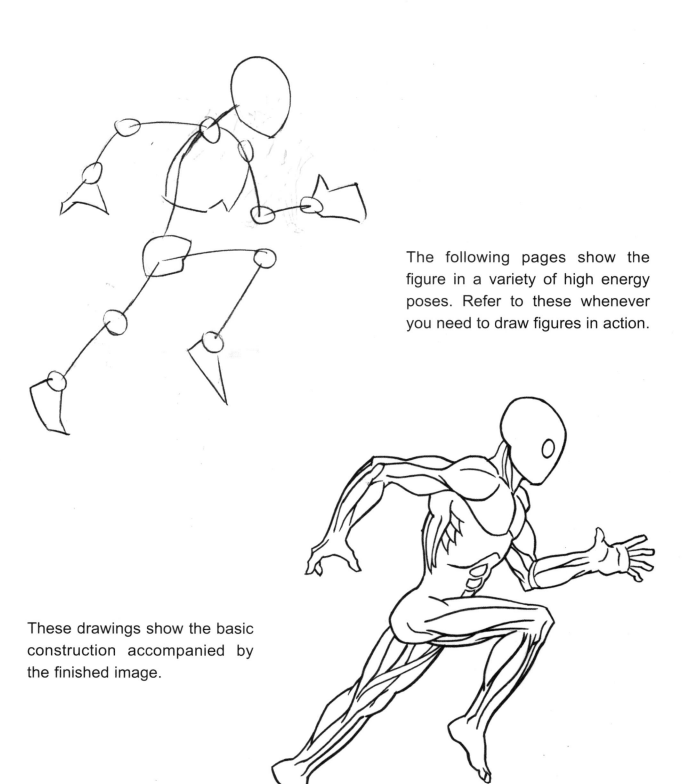

The following pages show the figure in a variety of high energy poses. Refer to these whenever you need to draw figures in action.

These drawings show the basic construction accompanied by the finished image.

Note how this figure remains balanced when the legs are drawn far apart. The weight is mainly on the his right leg, while the left leg keeps the figure balanced.

POW!

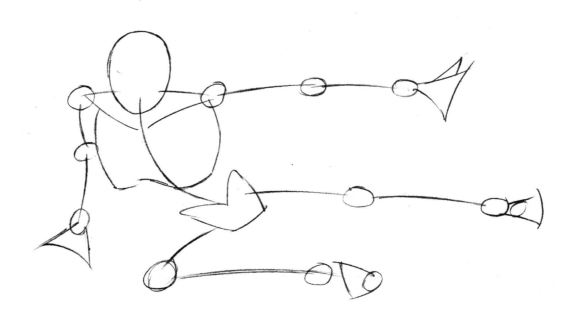

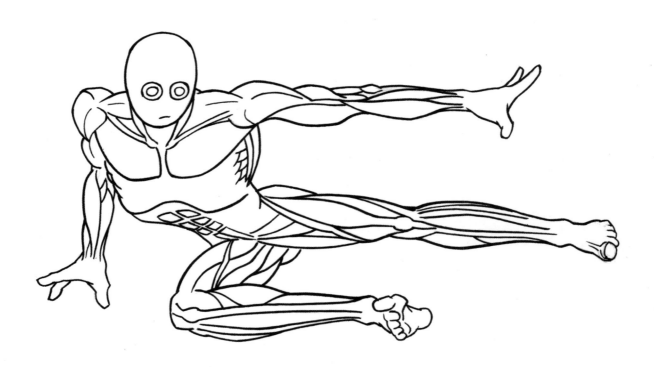

LINES OF ACTION

The simple diagram left shows the dynamics at work in the illustration on the opposite page. The figure being kicked away is forming a 'U' shape. The point of impact, his midriff, is dragging the rest of his limp body out of shot. Conversely, the other figure is forming a much tighter shape, with his left leg pointing in the direction of the flying body.

You can break all figure drawings down to these most basic lines. Have a look at some of your favourite artist's figure work and break the figures down to these most basic lines of action. Remember that simplicity is the key to good dynamic figure drawing. If you can't break it down to just a couple of simple lines, chances are your drawing will lack strength and dynamism.

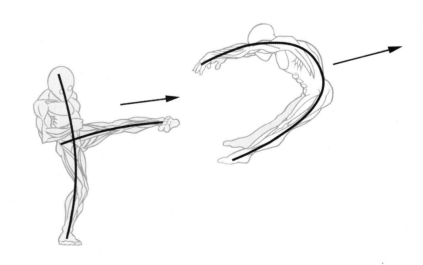

USING LINES OF ACTION: FINAL RESULT

Many people, succesful comic artists included, have not spent enough time learning how the various muscle groups are assembled and work together.

A fun game to play in your local comic book store is 'Spot the Fake Anatomy'. Signs to look for are lashings of unnecessary lines resulting in an outbreak of multiple triceps or double shoulders.

Fine, if all you want to do is draw pictures of people pounding the daylights out of each other, but pretty useless when you're asked to do something with a little more subtlety and expression.

Finding out how your own body works will always strengthen your work and make it that much more convincing.

If you have the time, get yourself down to your local life drawing class. It's always time well spent.

CHAPTER 4

DRAWING THE
HUMAN HEAD

DRAWING THE HEAD

The head, or more specifically the face, is the most expressive part of the human, or non-human body. It's the emotional center of our bodies, used to communicate rage, sadness, boredom, joy and a huge range of other feelings.

Whether it's a mouth screaming in pain or the subtlety of a lightly raised eyebrow, every manga artist should be armed with enough knowledge of the head's construction to enable them to depict the whole range of emotions.

THE MANGA HEAD

There are many, many varieties of head shape and size in manga, from realistic heads through to heads almost bigger than the character's body. Perhaps the most common is the 'squashed' head, which resembles that of a doll's head.

This shape is the one used when drawing characters with much larger-than-life eyes. Because the head shape has more 'width' it allows room for big eyes without crowding the face. Noses and mouths tend to be tiny on this shaped head – there isn't really any room for anything bigger.

THE SKULL

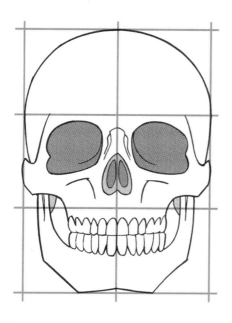 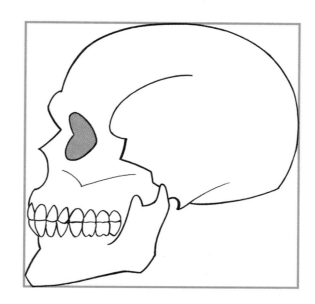

The human skull is made up of two bones, the jawbone and the cranium. The jawbone is attached by a loosely fitting hinge-type joint. Front on, the skull has a ratio of 3:2 height to width. In profile, its edges sit just within a perfect square.

HEY!

MY BRAIN BOX IS MUCH MORE MANGA-LIKE. MY PROPORTIONS ARE CLOSER TO A 2:2 RATIO — MORE LIKE A CUBE.

BASIC CONSTRUCTION OF A FEMALE HEAD

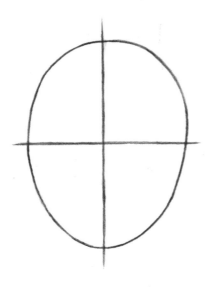

Step 1: Draw an oval and a line halfway down from left to right. This will be the eye line. Add a vertical line straight down the middle. We need this line to keep our face symmetrical.

Step 2: Add another horizontal line one third of the way down the bottom half of the oval.

Add the two curved lines at the points shown. This forms our jawline.

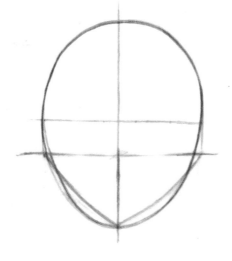

Step 3: Now for some eyes. Draw an oval inside a circle on the center line.

We'll erase the circles when our eyelids are established.

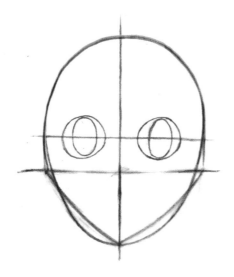

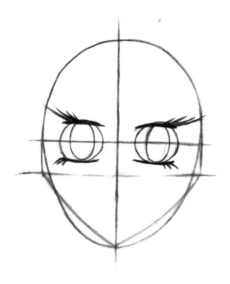

Step 4: Let's get some detail into those eyes. Start with the eyelids. Draw a slightly curved line over each eye as shown. Then sketch in the eyelashes. The angle of the eyelashes should get longer as they move outwards.

Step 5: Draw two more ovals inside our first ovals. Then add some highlights using small circles.

Fill the pupils in black, being careful to pick out the highlights.

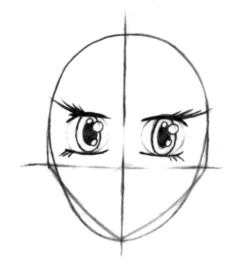

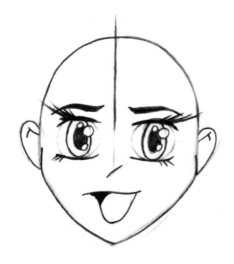

Step 6: The last facial features are the nose, mouth, ears and eyebrows.

These should be kept quite simple. Generally, don't bother adding teeth or gums except perhaps in close-up shots.

Step 7: Now let's cure our character of baldness.

You can add any kind of hair you like here. Try to use some light and dark shades to give the hair some body.

We'll discuss hair in more detail a little later in this chapter.

BASIC CONSTRUCTION OF A MALE HEAD

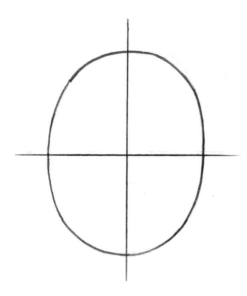

Step 1: Start as you did with our girl character, establishing your vertical and horizontal lines.

Step 2: We'll jump a stage here and get straight to the basic facial features.

No eyelashes for our boy.

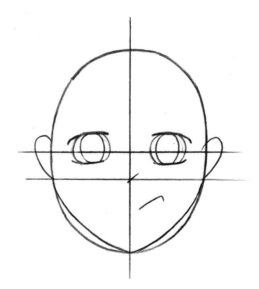

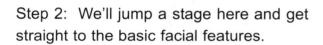

Step 3: Add the pupils and eye highlights as before followed by eyebrows and finally hair.

Don't fill in your blacks until you've got everything in place.

Add some highlights to the hair and then we're ready to fill in the black areas.
Easy, no?

A brief recap for girls versus boys:
Girls have thick eyelashes, lighter eyebrows and usually more extravagant hair and eyes.
Boys don't have eyelashes and have generally tougher features.

FROM AN ANGLE

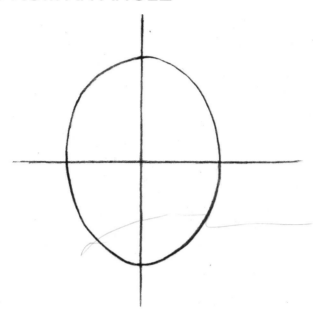

Step 1: We'll start as we did with the previous heads.

One oval, and bisecting horizontal and vertical lines.

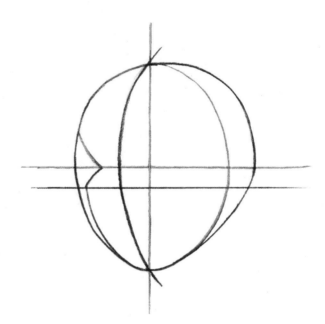

Step 2: If we think of the head as a sphere, this means our new center line should now be a curve.

Brow, cheek and jawline are drawn from the eye and nose lines.

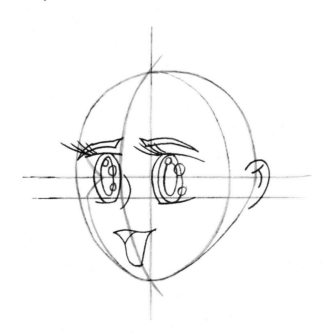

Step 3: See how the features have swung round with the new center line?

Draw the nose and mouth using the new center line as a guide. Then add the eyes at either side. Let's have an ear, too.

Step 4: The hair is based on the previous finished drawing of the girl. You don't need to be too fussy about this – hair changes shape constantly – just make sure it roughly resembles your previous version.

A three-quarter view is not easy to get right first time. If you're struggling, try simplifying the face as much as possible, then work your way up, adding more detail as your confidence improves.

The hair type we choose for our characters can have a massive impact on not just their appearance but their personality too. The following five drawings are all exactly the same except for the hairstyle.

Long, short, dark, light – experiment and see how it can radically change your character's personality.

A 'bunches' hairstyle, as above, is extremely unlikely to be worn by a grown woman. This immediately gives us some indication of the character's likely age.

'Bob' hairstyles are more typical of teenage manga.

Long, flowing hair is more readily associated with magical stories.

GIRLS AND WOMEN: THE DIFFERENCE

Girls are usually cuter, with more emphasis on their eyes. If you think of a baby's face, a woman's face is at the opposite end of the scale (no 'puppy fat') and a girl's will lie somewhere in-between.

Compare the two images here. A woman's features should be less cute and more elegant. Her facial features will be better defined.

If you want your character to look much older, try adding lines under the eyes.

EYES

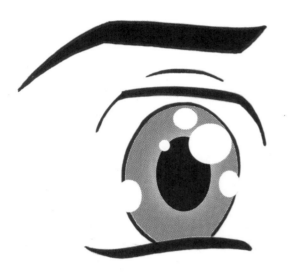

Male

Here's a pair of manga eyes in close up. It should be immediately obvious which eye belongs to which gender.

Manga artists have made a particular art of embellishing the eye, making it look almost liquid with multiple highlights and use of graduated tone.

Eyes are arguably the most expressive part of the body. In manga they come in a multitude of styles.

When drawing female eyes we should make a lot more of the eyelashes.

The size of our pupils changes according to our emotional state. We can use this to widen our vocabulary of expression.

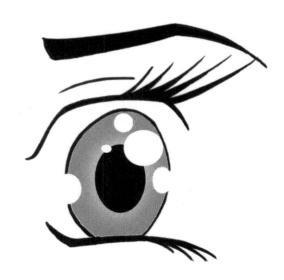

Female

Big pupils represent passion and other excited states. We can make characters look more distant and aloof by making their pupils smaller. To get real fear or excitement across we make the eyelids bigger than the pupils.

One of the real hallmarks of a certain type of manga is the extreme use of highlights or light reflections on a character's eye. These add great life and depth.

NOSES

The following diagrams show the geometric construction of the nose.

Remember that the bridge of the nose, the narrow part at the top, forms part of the eye sockets.

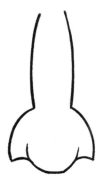

Usually, very little attention is paid to the nose when drawing manga characters.

There are quite a few exceptions though and we ought to be able to draw the nose if the occasion warrants.

Right is an 'upshot' of the nose, useful for when a character is looking down on you.

DRAWING HEADS FROM BEHIND

One of the most common mistakes when starting out is drawing the back of the head. Simple enough you'd think, but those ears can give us some real problems.

To the left is a typical example of how not to draw an ear. The artist just doesn't have the information to make the ear look remotely convincing.

Here, however, the ear is drawn as it should be: basically in two parts and pointing out rather than in.

It's worth taking the time to draw ears from different angles as they are one of the main indicators of the head's position.

There's an almost inexhaustible variety of head shapes and treatments in manga. Here's a few examples of the variety of possible styles.

CHAPTER 5

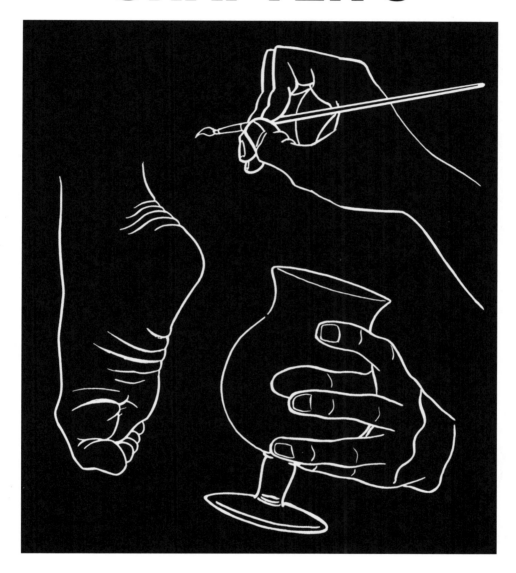

HANDS AND FEET

PART 1: THE HUMAN HAND

This image shows the main joints found in the human hand.

Point A is not actually a hand joint but does protrude in much the same way as a knuckle.

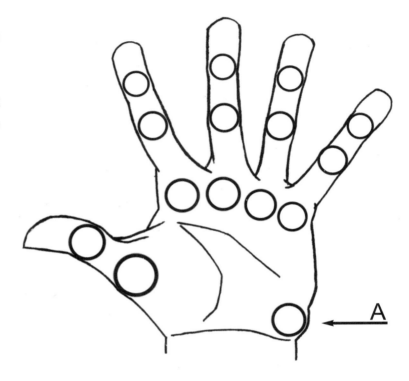

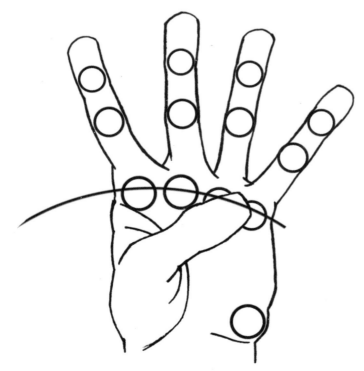

The thumb is more flexible than the fingers. It swings in an arc from the position shown above as far as the knuckle on the little finger.

Hands, along with the eyes and mouth, are the most expressive part of the human body. They are also probably the part of the body that give developing artists the most trouble.

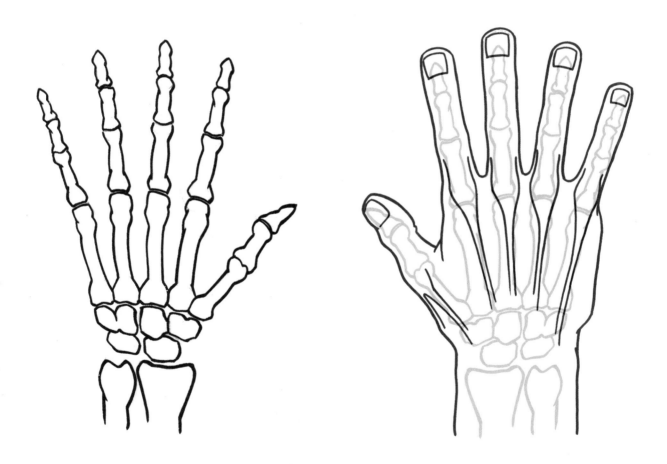

Above is the hand in both its skeletal form and its flesh form. The tendons on the back of the hand run from the knuckles over the wrist and into the major tendons of the arm.

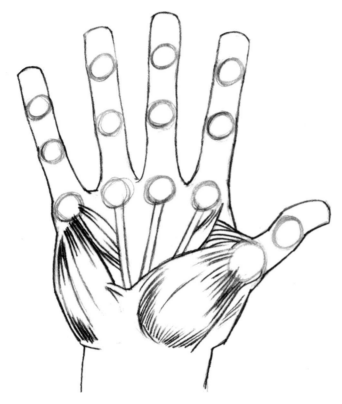

Here we have the front (palm) view and (below) the back view...

...but this time with muscle added.

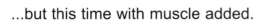

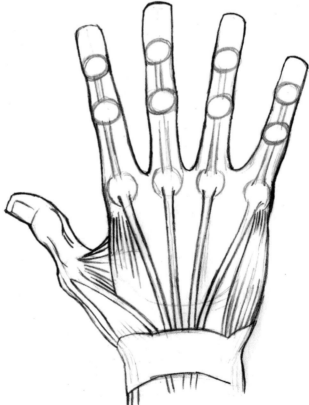

The male hand tends to have thicker fingers and of course shorter nails.

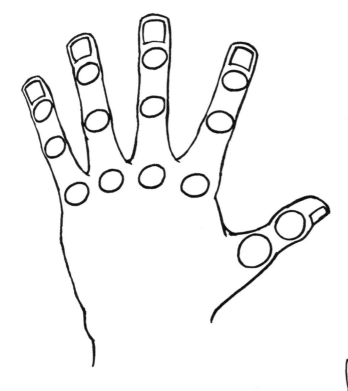

The female hand is proportionally smaller and the fingers more elongated.

DRAWING A FIST

When drawing a fist or clenched hand, forget about individual fingers. When the hand is clenched the fingers should 'fuse' to form an overall shape.

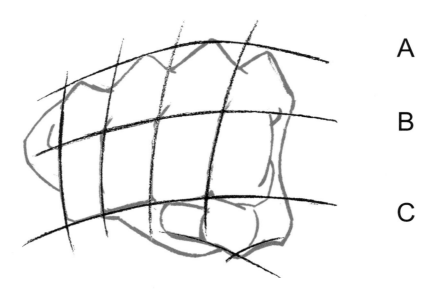

A

B

C

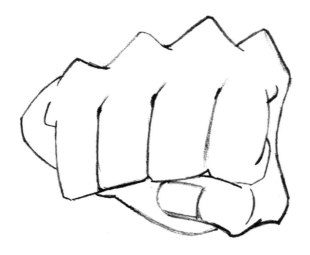

Draw some rough lines that represent the points A, B, and C, intersect them through the dip in the knuckles and roughly put in the angle of the thumb.

This will give your drawing structural strength and avoid fussiness or weakness in your final drawing.

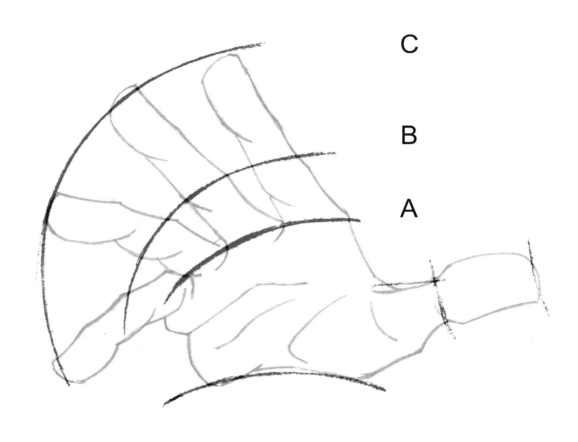

C

B

A

We can use the same basic idea when drawing more complicated hand shapes.

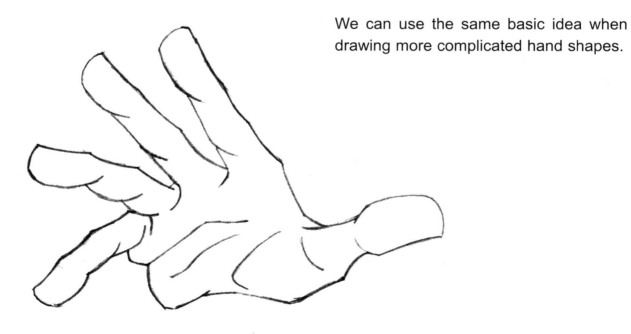

How the fingers relate to each other and act as a group is an important part of our understanding of the hand. The individual fingers seldom act completely independently. An exception is the classic 'pointing finger'. However, this only emphasizes the grouping of the other three.

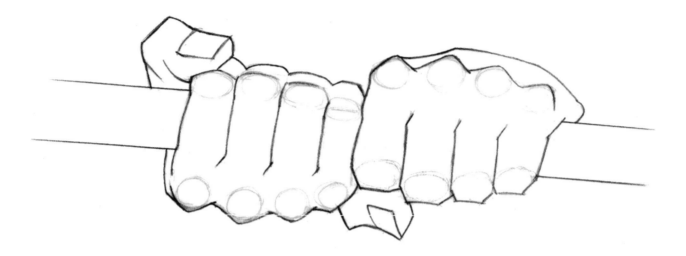

Correctly positioned thumbs are among the hardest things for the budding artist to master. They seem to defy all logic, as they are positioned at an entirely different angle to the fingers.

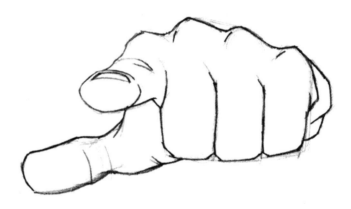

You have to remember that the thumb 'swings' in an arc towards and away from the palm.

...cheers.

PART 2: THE HUMAN FEET

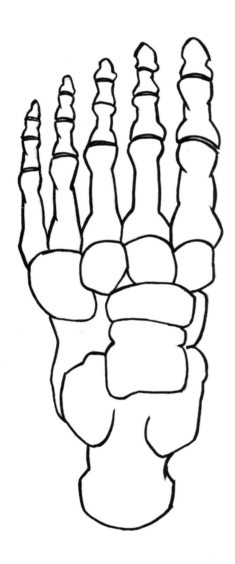 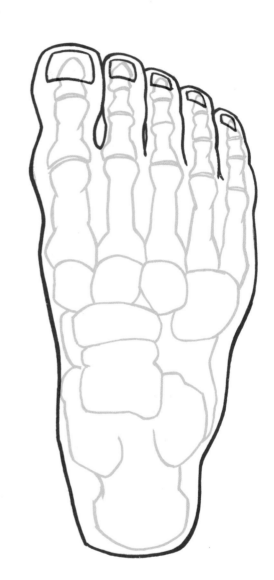

Most of the time, feet we have to draw are covered by shoes. But I'm afraid this does not excuse us from learning how the foot is constructed!

Here's the foot's skeletal structure.

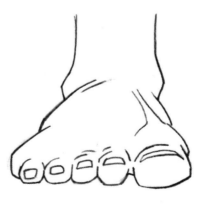

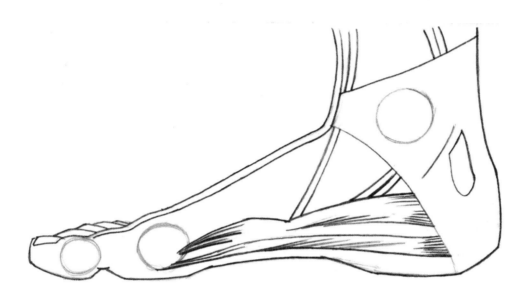

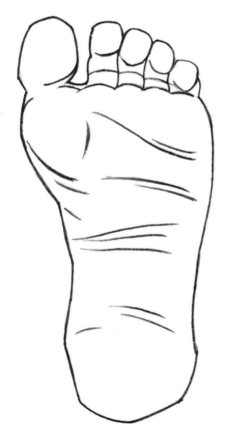

The top and bottom of the feet are of very different construction. Almost all of the foot's muscle is located at the sole, whereas the top of the foot is largely bone and tendon.

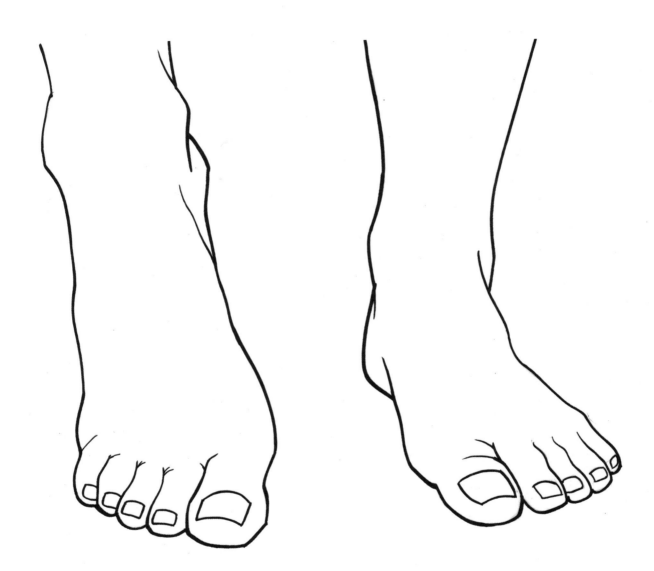

Okay, five toes – we know that much. But think of the big toe as one unit and the other four as another. The four toes almost never move any other way but all together.

Handled correctly the feet can be very expressive. They're stamped on the ground when we're angry and are at their most expressive when we dance.

Martial arts magazines are a great source of reference for expressive feet. With a wide variety of kicks and stances we can learn a lot very quickly from studying them.

Here is an image of the tendons of the foot. They run from the toes up through the ankle and into the leg. Bear in mind that you hardly ever see more of the tendons than is shown here.

Although bare feet are not often seen in manga, especially compared to hands, shoes are another matter. You will see shoes in roughly every other panel and they are surprisingly tough to get right.

Why should something as simple as a shoe be so hard to draw? For the simple reason that the entire human body is supported by them. When feet and shoes are drawn badly it may look as though your character is either falling over or has a broken ankle.

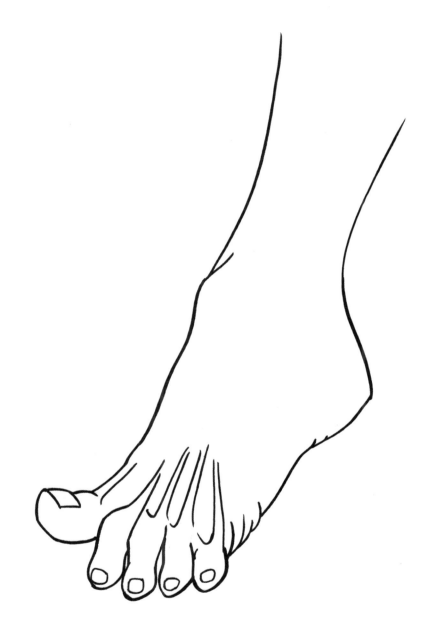

The bulk of the weight of the body rests on the heel when we stand and its shape is ideally suited for this – tapering out from the ankle to a wider, flat bottomed surface.

When a person is standing with their feet together, the heel should be in a direct line below the ear. This will ensure your character will look balanced.

Above is the most simple form of shoe. It may be boring, but it's a great shoe to test drive our drawing skills. In essence it's just a wrapping for the foot with a hard underneath. No heel and no laces to trip us up as we hone our shoe-drawing skills.

If we're having particular trouble drawing even a simple shoe in various positions, try the construction method below: a medium oval, a larger oval and a sphere take the place of the main components of the foot. Simplified like this, it's much easier to draw the foot at any angle we want – even from directly overhead.

Notice how the heel does not go straight down to the ground. It helps to add extra balance when the base of the heel is slightly further back.

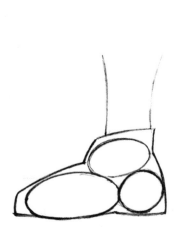
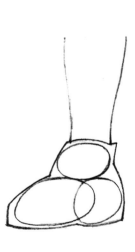

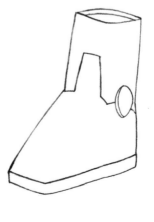

Robot boots and trainers aren't so very different from each other – the principles of shape and balance are the same.

The elegance of a woman's dress shoe is achieved by heavy emphasis of the foot's natural contours. Clogs and mules are much the same as the simple shoes on the previous page. The obvious difference is that the toe has been left off.

CHAPTER 6

TEXTILES AND
CHARACTER DESIGN

CHARACTER DEVELOPMENT AND CLOTHING

We've got the bones. We've got the flesh. But we can't have our characters walking around naked. Well, okay, we can, but sooner or later they're going to need some clothes. This is the chapter where we look at cotton, leather and other fabrics in order to help us decide what's right for our characters. We'll also look at fabric patterns and accessories.

As well as this, we'll take a look at character design and development to make sure they're absolutely ready before we send them out into the wider world of manga.

WHERE'S THE WARDROBE?

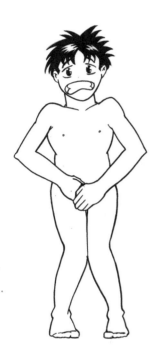

Ryuchi and Mayumi are feeling a little underdressed right now.

Let's get some basic clothes for them to hide their embarrassment.

SUITABLY DRESSED?

We managed to find something more or less suitable for Ryuchi, at least he seems happy enough. Mayumi's not too pleased with her outfit though – and who can blame her? Maybe if she was the skinny, leggy type it would work.

Just as with hair, a character's clothes make a massive impact on our perception of them. We can't just throw the first thing we think of on our characters.

HEY – THIS WORK SUIT IS KINDA COOL...

LUCKY YOU.

85

FABRIC

Clothing isn't a rigid unchanging suit that looks the same in any situation. It will bend, stretch, crease, fold and do any number of other things depending on gravity, force or even the weather.

The above image shows an extreme example of the effect of gravity on fabric. Let's have a closer look...

The unfortunate character thrashing around in mid-air is being dangled by his own shirt-collar. See how the lines leading down from the big guy's fingers to the little guy's shoulders are absolutely straight? This tells us that quite a lot of weight is being exerted on the fabric, with any more pressure it would probably start to rip.

The area under the arms and around the shoulders is 'bunching up', telling us there's a lot of pressure in this area. If the little guy's shirt was tucked in before, it certainly isn't now – the upward force has pulled it out of his trousers. It's also tugged the arms of his shirt almost up to the elbow.

To correctly render drapery we need to consider *where the force is being exerted*. There's usually something which is pulling, twisting or flattening the fabric.

JUDO THROW

Here's another good, if extreme example of the effects of pulls and twists on fabric. The guy on the right is trying to execute a fine judo throw using his opponent's sleeve and foot to throw him down. The stress lines tend to point to the main areas of force.

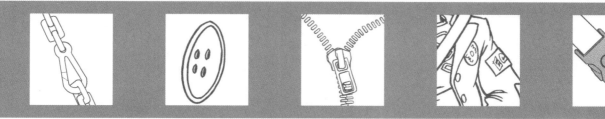

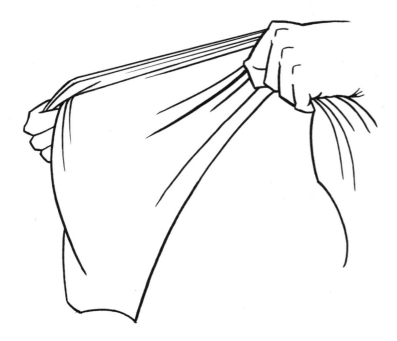

So far we've looked at thinner, cotton-type material.

Because it's light, cotton tends to produce a lot of stress lines, as shown in the illustration on the left.

Leather, on the other hand, is much thicker, preventing the material from forming more than one or two stress lines.

You'd get a similar result with a heavy blanket or other thick woollen items.

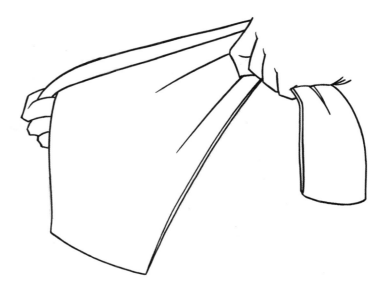

ADDITIONAL DETAIL

Once we've decided the type of material our character's clothes are going to be made from and the kind of clothes they're going to wear, we can start thinking about embellishments and accessories. These can include logos, patches, handbags and chains. Fashion magazines are an excellent source of material if you're stuck for ideas.

Decorations and accessories are a great way to give extra shape and contours to your character as well as making them more visually appealing. Don't go totally over the top though – when you have to draw that character for 40 panels you'll soon regret smothering him in acres of excessive detail.

The golden rule applies here – keep things as simple as your character's needs dictate. Put too much clutter on your character and they'll fail to stand out against detailed backgrounds.

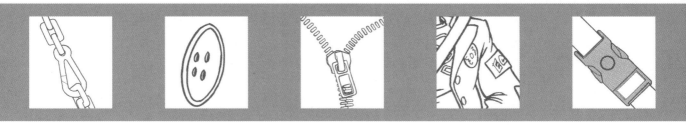

PATCHES AND PATTERNS

The character on the facing page has about as much detail and decoration on his upper body as is practical.

We could have added more detail to his bottom half, but it would have taken attention away from what we're already happy with.

Flat tone, stripes, checks, hoops – there's an almost unlimited range of patterns we can use to add personality to characters.

The pattern types on the character above are put on 'flat'. No attempt has been made to follow the contours of her body.

This gives our character more of a designer-look. It works well against backgrounds that uses strong geometric shapes and is less concerned with realism.

THE MATERIAL

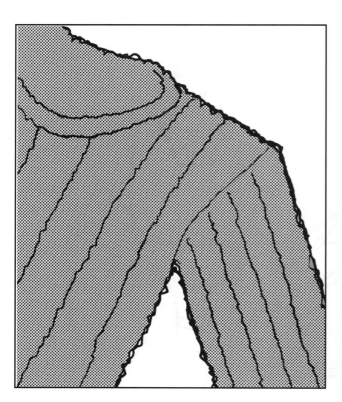
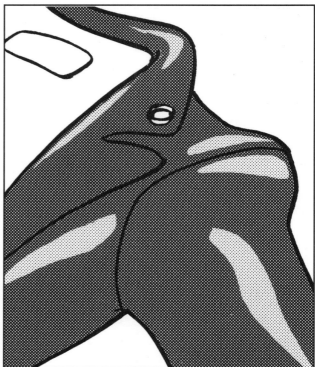

Above are two very different materials. On the left is wool. As it's very fuzzy, it absorbs rather that reflects light. This means there are no reflections and very little in the way of highlights. This type of material is generally rendered very 'flat' – usually in just one color.

Denim, felt and toweling all have low-reflectivity and should be rendered in a neutral tone. If the material is soft then keep the contrast down. For hard materials increase the contrast.

On the right is leather. This material is much more light-reflective and should be drawn with high contrast. The dark areas are very dark and reflected light is close to pure white. Other highly reflective materials include plastics, metal armour and rubber.

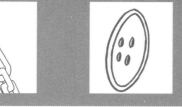

Pictured right is probably the ultimate in highly reflective clothing.

This body suit, made of rubber, only shows either black or white, with no other shades in-between. It's a great material for drawing our more shapely characters in.

When handling highlights in this type of material, they should always pick out the contours of the person's body. You should only pick out those parts of the body which face the light source. In the case of this image the main reflected areas are the breasts, the upper legs and a bit of the tummy. This tells us that the light source comes from directly above.

Try to imagine how she would be lit if our light source was coming from the right hand side.

To give extra emphasis to her clothing and hair, we've toned her skin and her gun and put her against a dark background. This leaves her dress and hair highlights to stand out.

CHARACTER DESIGN AND DEVELOPMENT

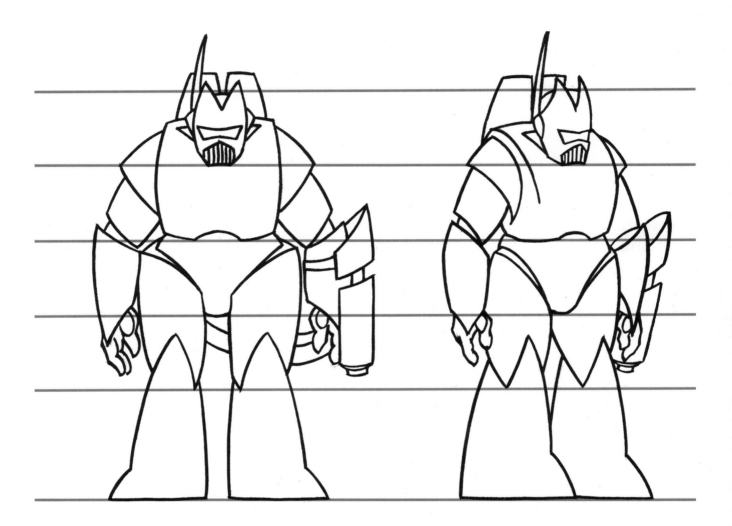

Before we start drawing a major story we have to give ourselves the best chance we can of keeping all the various elements consistent. Inconsistency will only distract the reader and spoil their enjoyment of the story. It will also give us major headaches when we can't get our character to look correct at certain angles.

Here's the solution: as mentioned in chapter 2, no anime film is started until all the characters have what are known as 'turnarounds' or 'character rotations'. The same principles should apply to our manga.

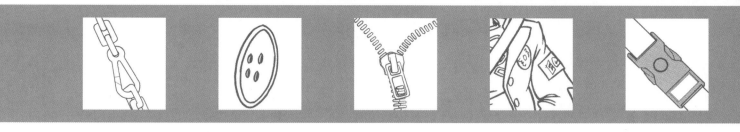

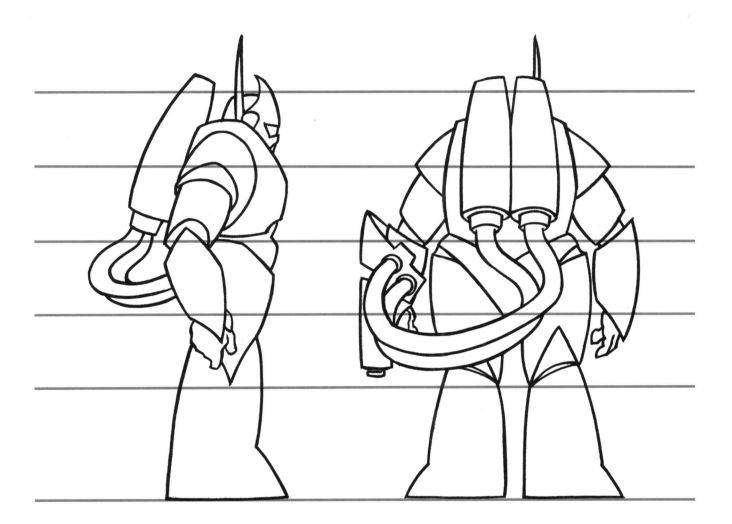

Across these two pages you can see the turnaround for the cyborg character Gogos. Back, front, side and three-quarters are the minimum number of positions for our turnaround to be useful.

Drawing turnarounds is a useful exercise in itself. They force us to address any weak spots in our structure. If you're having trouble drawing yours, try breaking the character down into easier-to-handle geometric shapes. There's more about that coming up in chapter 8.

GOGOS IN ACTION

Now our character's form is established from all angles, we can start to have fun with him. We'll draw him from several different angles, knowing that we have the information we need to do so.

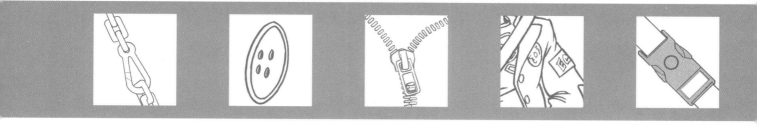

MUNITIONS FACTORY

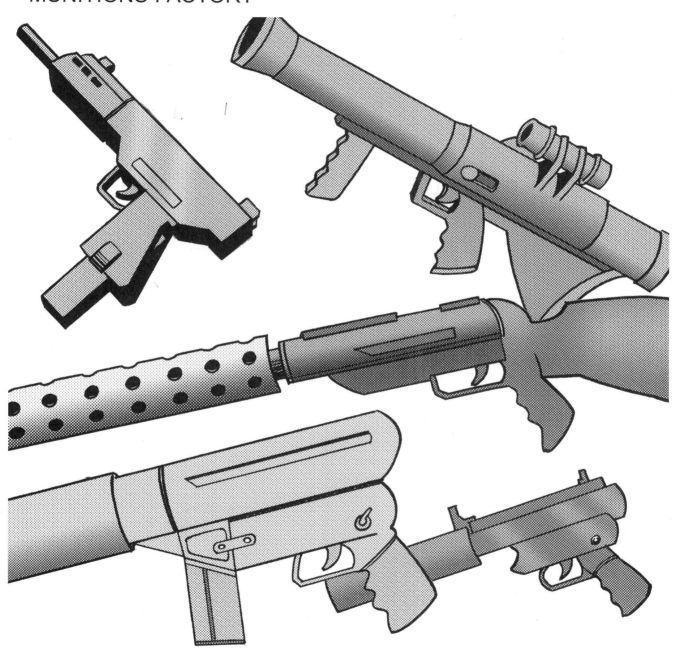

Guys like Gogos don't tend to walk around unarmed. Weapons to blast your enemies with come in many shapes and sizes. Above is a selection of handy, ready-to-use firepower.

CHAPTER 7

NON-HUMAN
CHARACTERS

NON-HUMAN CHARACTERS

Now that we've got our human characters constructed and dressed we need to take a look at other classes of character. Every non-human falls into this category, from pet cats to giant killer robots.

Let's break them into three types:

ANIMALS

Cats, dogs, whales, frogs, worms – they have all featured in manga somewhere. Sooner or later you're going to have to draw them.

ROBOTS, ANDROIDS AND CYBORGS

These refer to various types of human impersonators central to futuristic strips. They are either part human or based on human design.

SUPERNATURAL CHARACTERS

These are usually humanoid characters – often from another dimension. The evil ones enjoy treating humankind like their personal playthings.

DRAWING ANIMALS

There's an almost infinite range of creatures and beasts that have the potential to appear in our manga.

What makes one animal different from another? What particular attributes do they have?

If we can get down to the essence of this, by focusing on the key characteristics, our animals will be much stronger for it.

These simple drawings illustrate what I mean. They are an attempt to capture the essence of animals with a minimum number of lines.

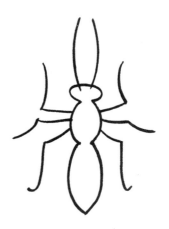

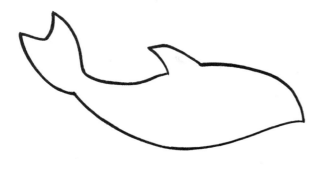

DOGS AND OTHER MAMMALS

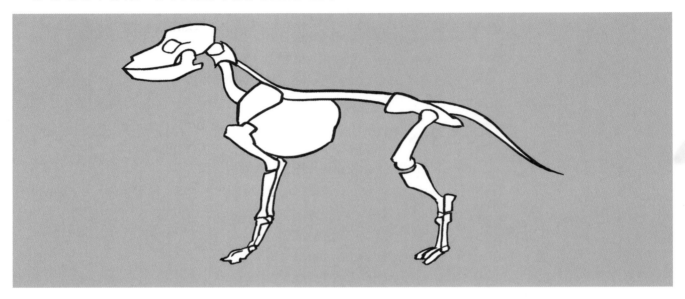

One of the most common animal character types is a dog. Have a look at the simplified skeleton above and compare it with the human skeleton in chapter 2.

The main difference is obviously the fact that the dog is on all fours, but once we get past that, the skeletal structure is really similar.

The skull shape is very important to consider. Unlike us and primates, most other mammals have a snout — an elongation at the front of the skull.

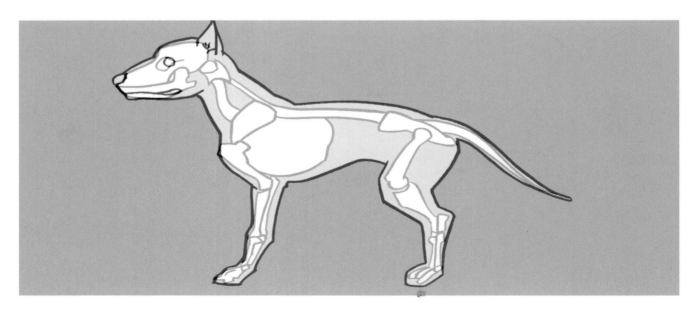

CATS VERSUS DOGS

There's a phrase, coined by the famous designer, Walter Gropius, that can also tell us a lot about the differences between mammals: 'Form follows function'. It means this: the body type of any animal depends on its behavior.

A dog is essentially a scavenger. It will eat, or try to eat, almost anything. It has a wide range of teeth for both grinding and slicing its food.

A cat, on the other hand, is a hunter. It eats only meat and its body has to be sleek and flexible. Its teeth are primarily for tearing and cutting through meat.

Kitty actually has a hard time dealing with that dried food we feed him – his teeth are not really made for the job.

Try doing some sketches of cats to capture their shape. They are far more flexible and curvaceous than dogs.

103

REPTILES

More primitive in construction, reptiles are more cartilage than bone which makes them incredibly flexible.

As shown at the beginning of this chapter, a typical reptile is 's' shaped with a rounded triangle for a head.

The most basic reptile is a snake – a lizard without legs.

You can see this in the drawing to the left.

The word 'dinosaur' literally means 'terrible lizard' – terrible as in terrifying.

Crocodiles, alligators and Komodo dragons are the closest thing to these colossal creatures that we have left today.

The meat-eating dinosaurs were typical hunters, swift and deadly with highly flexible bodies.

The herbivorous ones were much slower and bulkier.

BUGS

Utterly unlike either mammals or reptiles, insects get their form not from a conventional skeleton but from an exo skeleton, which means they have natural armour-plating protecting their soft, squishy insides.

All insects have three main sections, although this is not always obvious. They are:

The head – eyes, mouth and antennae are found here.

The thorax – this is the section to which the legs and wings are attached.

The abdomen – where the insect digests its food, and if you're unlucky, the part with which it will sting you!

Insect construction has been borrowed for the design of alien creatures for decades. After all, what's more scary than a giant, super-powerful creepy-crawly?

Insects aren't alone in lending themselves to the design of new lifeforms, as the next page illustrates.

BRING ON THE CRUSTACEANS

Lobsters are really important in manga. Sound ridiculous? Well, it's not.

Not so much lobsters themselves, as the way their body armour is made.

If, instead of bone, we have a character with a super-tough inflexible exo skeleton, we'll have to design the joints very differently.

This is where we look to nature for the best solution.

Lobsters have swivel-type joints in their limbs, allowing them a fair degree of movement without compromising the effectiveness of their armour.

A small amount of movement in each joint but in different directions is enough to allow a lobster/armoured character to move one of its limbs anywhere it likes.

Compare the two drawings here. You'll never look at cyborg battle armour the same way again.

ROBOTS, CYBORGS AND ANDROIDS

Of the three types of mechanical humans, the robot is the type we can have more of a free reign with. Robots have only ever had to be loosely-based on the human form.

The golden age of robots was probably in the 1950s and 1960s. Since then, artificial lifeforms have become a lot more sophisticated. As a result, robots are rarely seen these days, except in deliberately retro strips.

Roughly speaking, a robot is artificial intelligence in a moving box. Its key features are either 'destruction and evil' or 'pathos and good'. Let's draw a few different types...

ANDROIDS

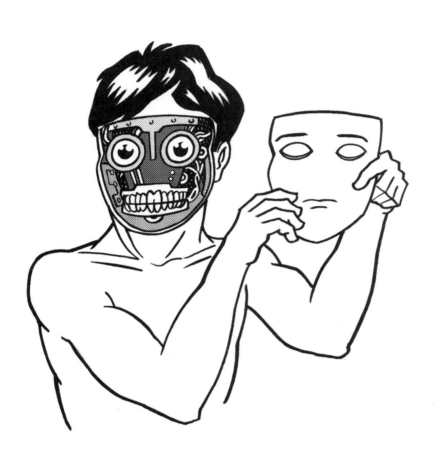

Unlike robots, androids are deliberately made to resemble humans.

The obvious difference is their mechanical brains and internal mechanisms.

Typical uses of androids would be as servants, either in domestic situations or in a military capacity.

Androids are also used for espionage, to get behind enemy lines without risking human life. It's also a waste of time torturing an android for information.

In manga, there is often some kind of visual clue that lets you, the reader, know you're not looking at a 'real' person.

CYBORGS

Once ordinary people, cyborgs are modified versions of ourselves.

They are half-human, half-machine creations, commonly found in the cyberpunk genre of manga.

They generally think and act like humans but often feature some obvious physical modifications.

Typically, a cyborg may have enhanced vision or hearing, or even some kind of brain implant. Some cyborgs walk around with someone else's memories in their heads.

Cyborgs are possibly the most popular type of character in futuristic manga. There's something about them that appeals to our imagination. Perhaps it's because we know that we are already at the stage with our technology where we can modify humans, at least in a small way. Technically-speaking, a person with a pacemaker fitted to their heart is actually a cyborg!

SUPERNATURAL CHARACTERS

These are largely, but not always, variations on the human form.

They can be creatures of pure evil, who have come to torment mere mortals. Also, they can be friendly, helpful spirits who use their magical powers to assist us.

How should we best portray pure evil? These are creatures without conscience, bent on destruction and causing pain and misery. It's no use portraying them in a nice sweater and sandals, we have to make them look like what they are: scary and powerful.

The supernatural world is one of extremes. So if we want to portray a spirit of pure goodness we have to get across those aspects of humanity that would be most prominent – namely love, compassion and a sense of righteousness.

If you are creating a new supernatural creature, you should observe the same rules as creating new animals. Always base them on something in reality, which you can then alter and twist to your character's particular needs.

CHAPTER 8

PROPS AND VEHICLES

MAN-MADE OBJECTS

So far we've had a good look at all aspects of drawing people, as well as non-human characters. But our manga is going to look pretty empty with just characters in it.

What we need now is an understanding of everyday objects that our characters can interact with and how these objects are constructed.

It is key to learn that all of these man-made items can be simplified. Whether we're drawing a chair or an express train we first need to break them down to their simplest forms. When we have their basic construction in place we can start to add detail that identifies the object.

The way we should do this is:
1. Decide the angle at which we want to draw the object.
2. Represent the object as simply as possible.
3. Add the detail that makes the object unique.

SIMPLE GEOMETRIC SHAPES

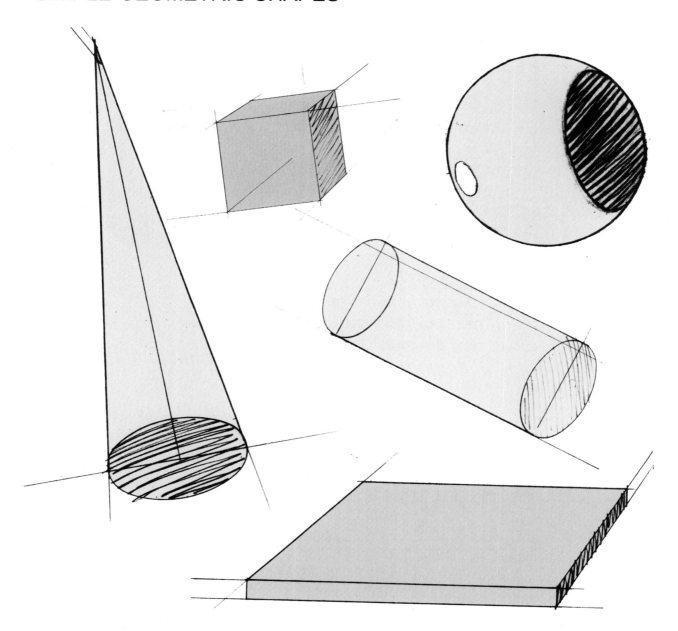

I know what you're thinking. Yawn, snore. You want to draw cars and bikes and I'm telling you about cones and cubes. But nearly all vehicles and everyday objects can be broken down into these basic shapes. This will help us understand their structure.

These commonplace objects are obvious examples of slightly modified, simple geometric shapes.

The tumbler is made from a cross-section of a cone, the billiard ball is simply a sphere, the dice is a rounded-off cube and the mug is a cylinder with a handle.

MORE COMPLEX SHAPES

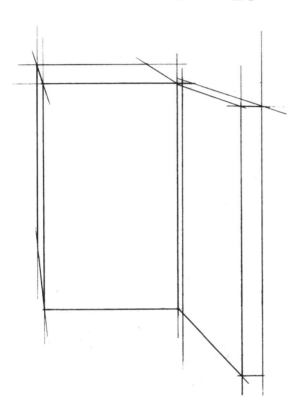

Here we have two boxes. One is quite deep, the other shallow.

It could represent a wide range of household objects: a wardrobe, a bathroom cabinet and so on.

In our case it represents a typical fridge.

A fridge is little more than a collection of smaller boxes inside a much larger one.

Don't worry about the perspective in this drawing. We'll get round to that in the next chapter.

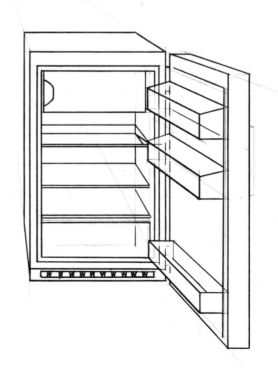

117

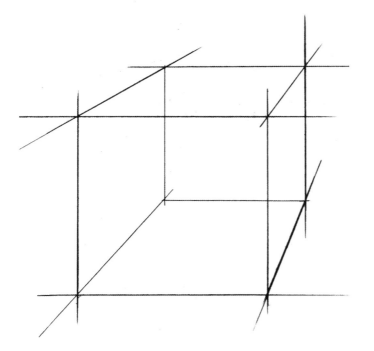

A square or near-square box like the one pictured left is probably the most common and useful tool in our construction kit.

A whole host of everyday objects is constructed from it by either adding to or subtracting some part.

Television sets, microwaves, and coffee tables are just some of the everyday objects which use a box for their basic construction.

This armchair (right) is the above box with one section for the seat, back and arms cut-out and another section for the underneath and legs.

It's often more useful to see objects in this way, rather than as a collection of individual parts. This tells us more about their design and structure.

We'll see these same principles in action as we learn to draw vehicles.

DRAWING CARS 1

What is the underlying structure of a car? Even though car shapes have changed drastically in the last 10 years, their basic structure remains the same. A car is essentially a smaller box on top of a larger one, with four short cylinders underneath – you guessed it, these are the wheels.

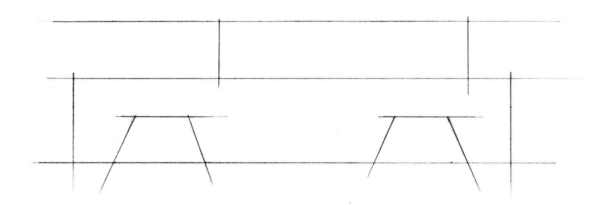

To illustrate this, we'll look at an average hatchback design from a side view:
The smaller box (on top) is approximately two-thirds the height of the bottom box. The bottom box is roughly five times as long as it is high. The tops of the wheel arches are slightly above half of the height of the bottom box.

Over this template we can then add the main features of the car.

Now let's erase the guidelines and add some more detail, such as wheel hubs and door handles.

Want to draw a sedan? Couldn't be easier! Just move the back window forward like so...

DRAWING CARS 2

Let's have a look at the same car, but this time from above. We can use the same proportions so we know we're getting it right.

Now all we need to do is get the width of the car right and then fill in the gaps, like so:

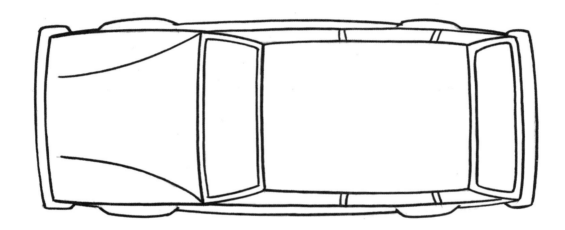

Easy, eh?

Let's quickly peek at the front and back ends:

Now we've got all the information we need, we can draw our car at any angle we please.

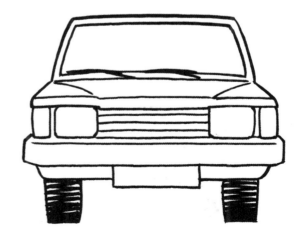

DRAWING TRUCKS

Trucks are usually even easier to draw than cars. Big box, small box. Six cylinders. That's it.

DRAWING PLANES

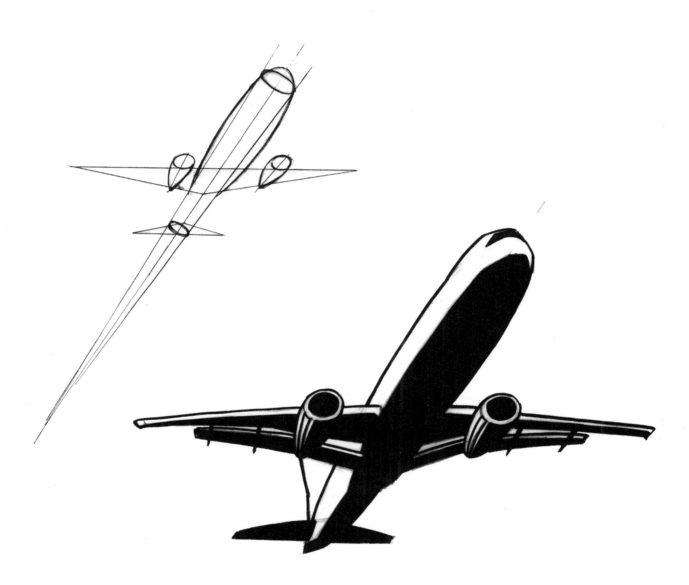

A plane is slightly more complex. The main section of the body is a tapered cylinder, with two smaller tapered cylinders for the jets. The wings and tail are triangles.

DRAWING TRAINS

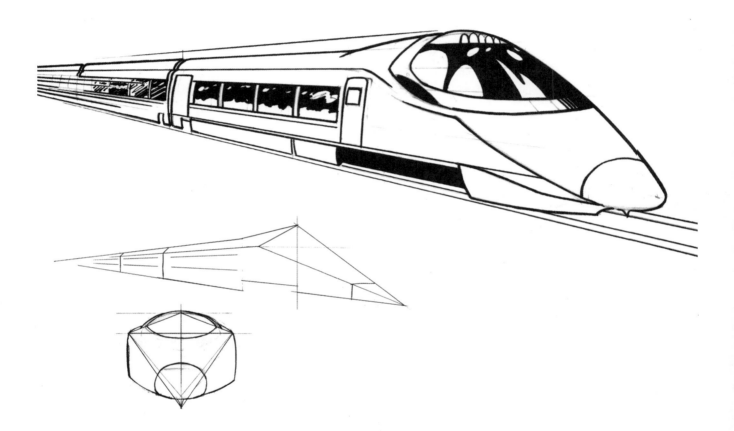

Trains are normally the simplest of the lot, except in this case. I thought we'd make it more interesting and draw a bullet train. Like all trains, the carriages are a collection of slightly modified oblongs.

The front section however is a little more complex.

This is a wedge shape – a little like a pyramid, designed to slice through the air as quickly as possible.

Remember that 'form follows function' line from the previous chapter? The same thing applies here too.

DRAWING MOTORCYCLES

Although we think of motorcycles as being simpler than the previous vehicles, they are actually harder to break down into simple geometric shapes.

The majority of modern bikes and the kind that are most often used in manga have large, streamlined fairings which obscure much of the front-end and the engine.

There are four main elements to the construction of a motorcycle.
They are: wheels, gas tank, seat and fairings. If we break it down in to these elements
we'll be able to organize its structure much more easily.

The overall 'look' of a modern bike is one of agression and speed. Look at the contours
in the illustration above to see this.

DRAWING A SPORTS CAR FROM A TOUGH ANGLE

Now for the most complex piece of vehicle drawing so far. Using the principles from the previous pages, we're going to draw a two-door sports car at a 3/4 angle.

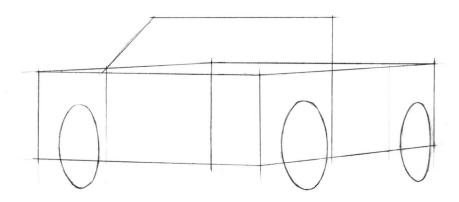

Step 1: The framework.
Draw the box as before, dividing it roughly into thirds at the side. Add the windshield at the first third (notice the perspective).

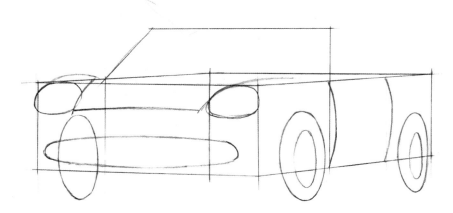

Step 2: Now add the hood line and grille.
Draw the sides of the hood by making an arc from the hood line to the bottom corners of the windshield.
Show the position of the lamps. These fit snugly between the sides of the hood and the original box. Loosely indicate the wheel hubs with a light outline.

Step 3: Now that we have the major parts in place, let's erase some of those guidelines.
Next we'll add the wheel arch, some wing mirrors and the recess for the lamps.
It's starting to look like a car now.

Step 4: Let's add some seats, give it some alloy wheels and a wing mirror. Remember –
the seats are a long way behind the windshield and so may be positioned further to the
right than you think.
We'll also put in the sunshields and add more detail to the lamps and the grille.
Lastly, put in the air vent (behind the door) and indicate a logo below the hood line.

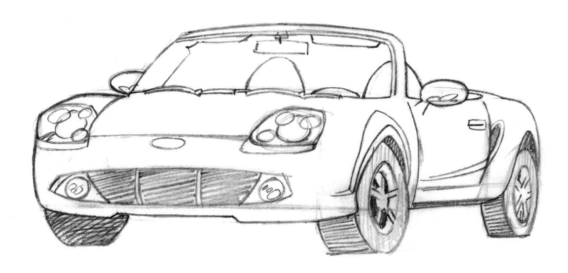

Step 5: We're nearly there – we'll add some wipers and generally tighten up a little before getting the ink out.

Step 6: You don't have to ink and tone the finished car – but if you do, it shouldn't look a million miles away from the above.

CHAPTER 9

ARCHITECTURE
AND PERSPECTIVE

PERSPECTIVE

BASIC ONE, TWO AND THREE POINT PERSPECTIVE

Although mankind has been making images since the days of living in caves, it's only in the last few hundred years that we've worked out the rules of perspective. Perhaps we didn't think it was important enough – after all, comic books didn't exist until the 20th century.

If we don't learn perspective our manga will look like something drawn in the Dark Ages.

We're going to be looking at three types of perspective, rising in complexity (and realism) as we go on.

You'll notice all the lines end at the *horizon line* (the point at which the curvature of the earth prevents us from seeing any further.) There can be one or many points on the horizon line that our perspective lines move towards. These points on the horizon are called *vanishing points* for obvious reasons.

The horizon line also represents our *eye level* i.e. where we place the horizon affects the kind of view we end up with. A low horizon will give us an 'ant's eye' view, a horizon line near or even above the top of our page will put the viewer up in the clouds.

ONE POINT PERSPECTIVE

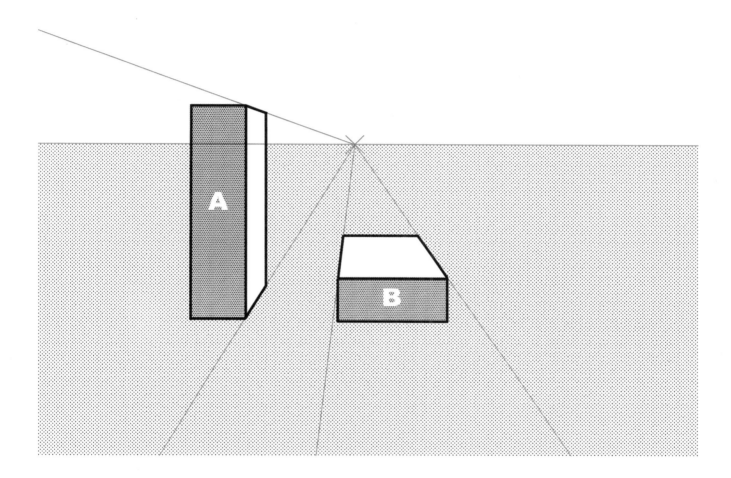

As the name suggests, perspective of this type is only concerned with one plane. As shown above, the lines that aren't directly facing us (i.e. they are not at right angles to each other) all move towards one vanishing point. This tells us something about the objects; they are *parallel* to each other (i.e. the distance between them is the same at either end).

So what happens if we rotate object B so it is no longer parallel with A?

TWO POINT PERSPECTIVE

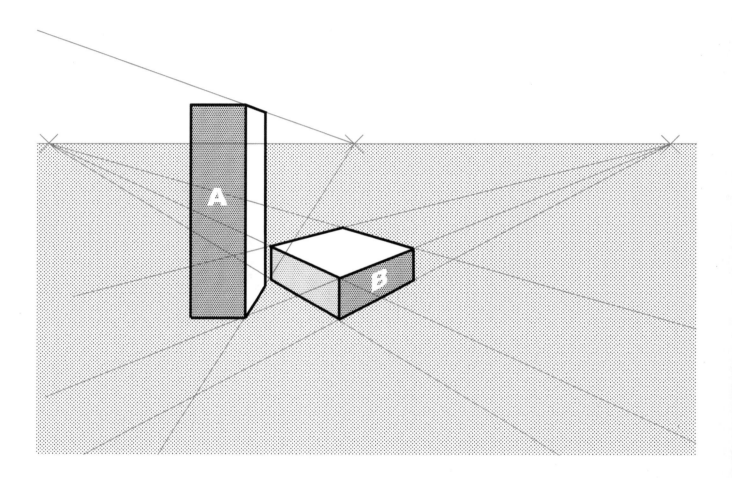

Okay, we've turned object B around so it's no longer facing in quite the same direction as A. This has effectively created two new vanishing points. If object A is still facing north then object B is now facing northwest.

Our drawing is starting to look more realistic already.

134

THREE POINT PERSPECTIVE

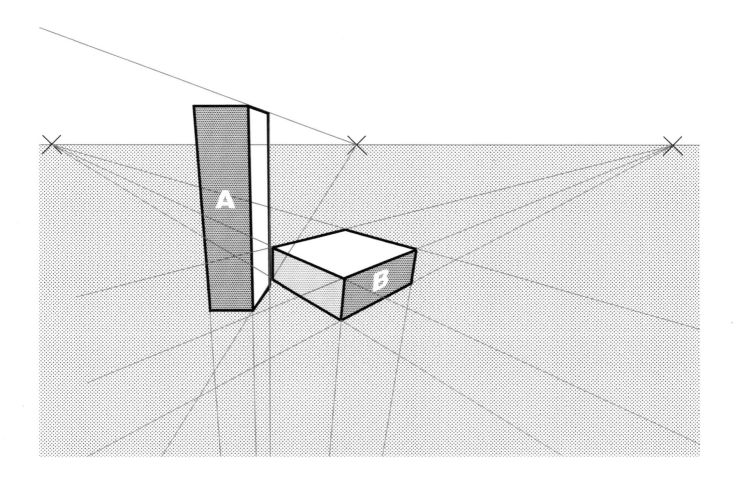

Just as we are always in front of or behind any three-dimensional object, we are also always either above or below it. With our high horizon line we're going to need the perspective of our blocks to get smaller as they move towards the center of the earth.

Of course I've exaggerated this effect; it's nearly always much more subtle than I've shown here. The exception is in 'wide angle' shots where this effect is emphasized for greater dynamic impact.

LOWERING OUR SIGHTS

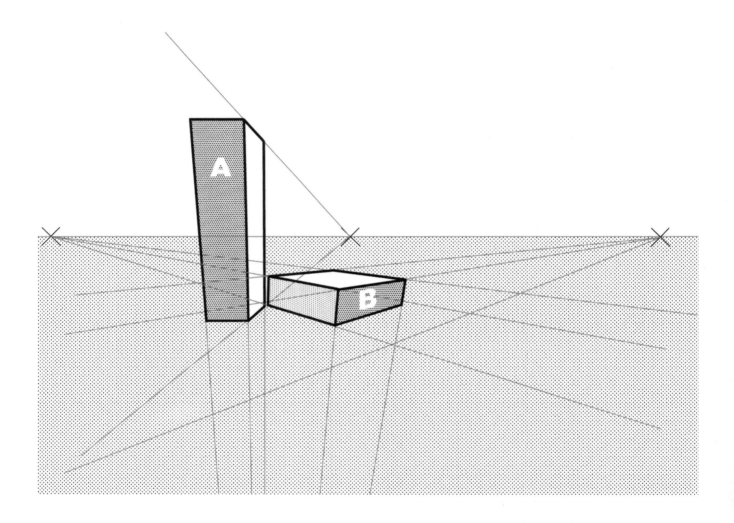

Above is what happens when we lower the horizon line. Everything else remains in exactly the same position, but now we feel much closer to the ground.

FOUR POINT PERSPECTIVE?
It is entirely possible to create a drawing that makes the viewer feel that they are looking up as well as down (and left and right). There will be an example of this a little later, but for now, let's put what we've learned to use.

DRAWING A TOWER BLOCK IN THREE POINT PERSPECTIVE

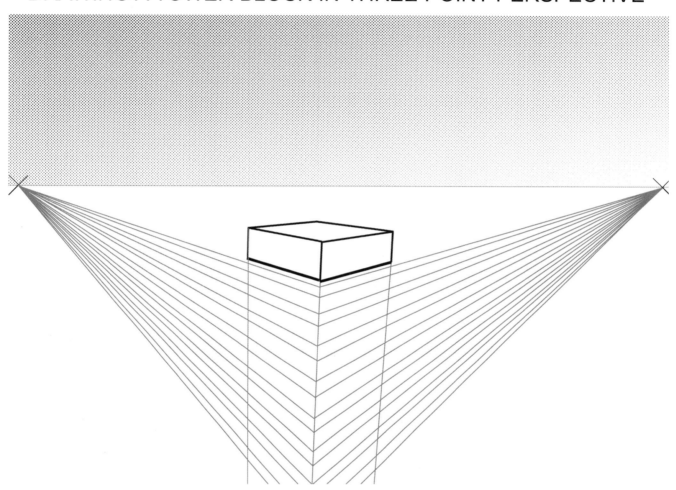

Step 1: Let's use our familiar block B as our starting point. This will form the roof of the tower. The image above shows the vanishing points. Using the two vanishing points we'll draw in the window and balcony sections.

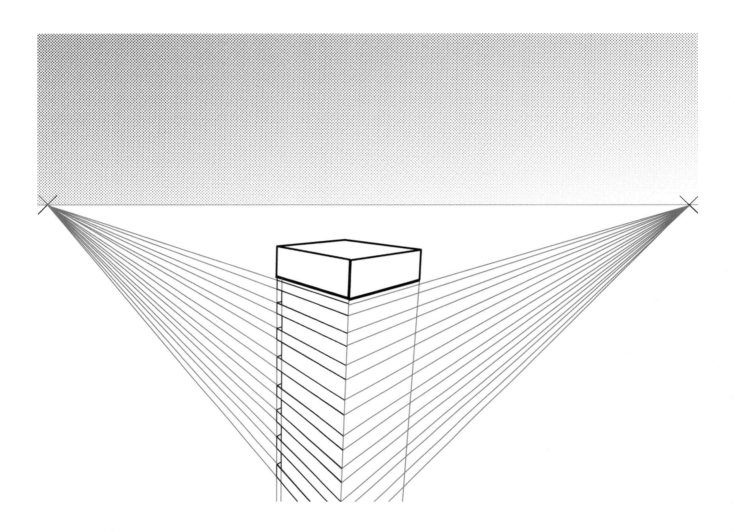

Step 2: When we've done the windows and balconies on both sides we need to put in some separate windows. But the windows are in perspective and they're set back from the balconies.

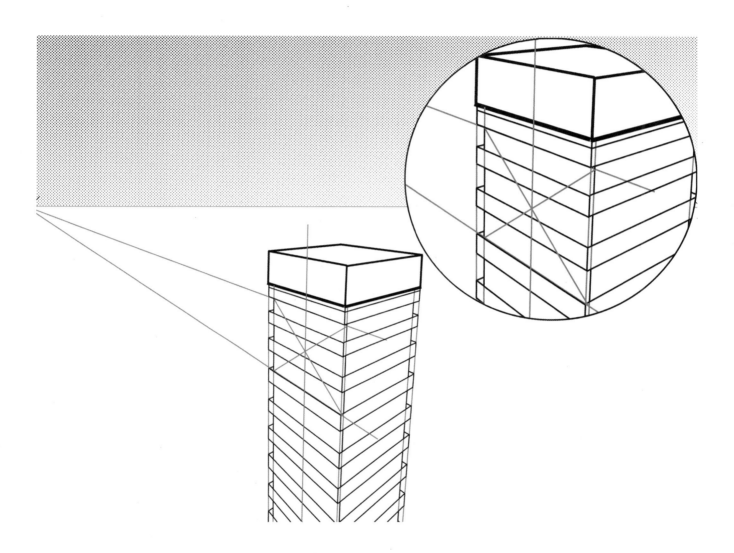

Step 3: We want to find the halfway point on the windows so let's use some basic geometry. We need to find one section of window which we can diagonally bisect. As the balcony obscures part of the window we first need to slightly extend the top and bottom right hand side (see above).

We now have a tidy rectangle representing the window in perspective. We'll draw two diagonal lines and run the vertical perspective line through it. Now we've found the center line of all the windows on that side of the building.

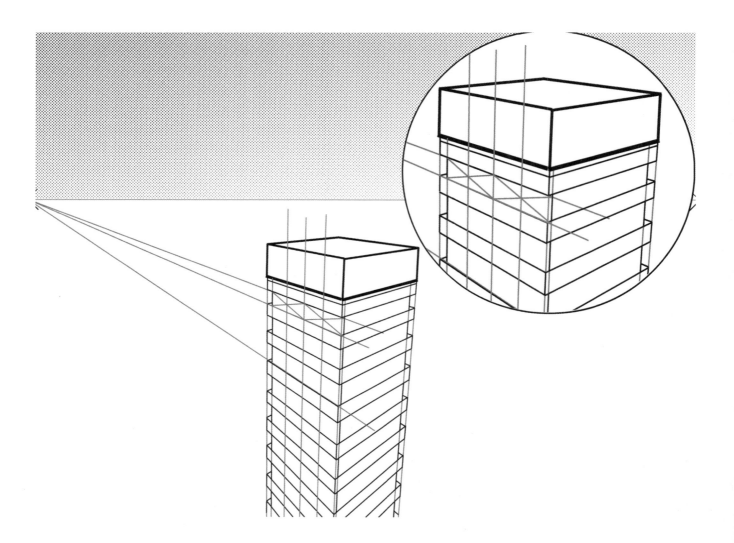

Step 4: But we want four windows, so let's repeat the procedure, using diagonal lines to bisect each of the two new windows, as above.

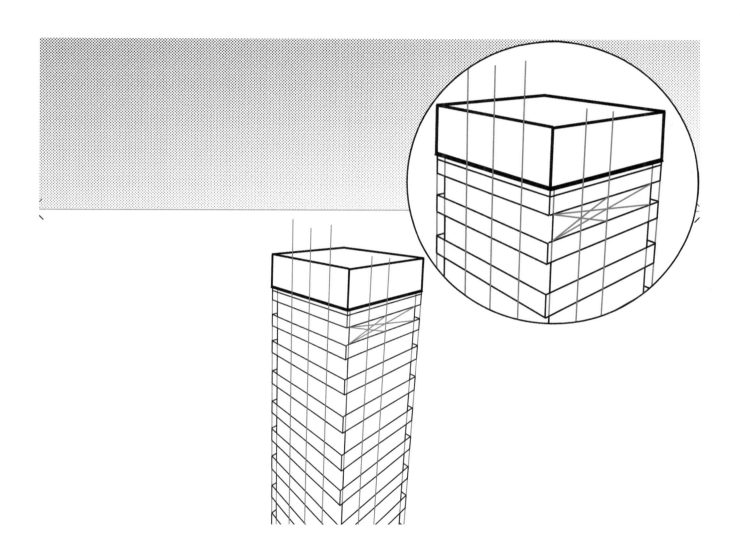

Step 5: Do the same procedure as in steps 3-4 on the other side of the building – it'll be easier as there's no balcony obscuring our rectangle window.

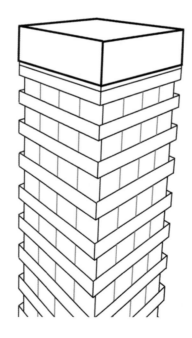

Step 6: You'll now be able to put in the windows in the knowledge that they are completely accurate.

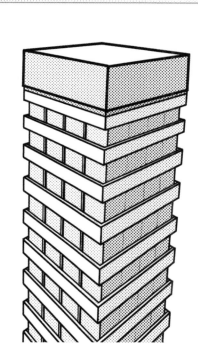

Step 7: We're almost done. Let's just finish off with some tone. Learn more about tone in chapter 11.

VISION IN FOUR DIRECTIONS

Remember I mentioned four point perspective? Here's an example of what I mean. You'll no doubt notice that none of the perspective lines are actually straight. And that's exactly how it is in reality too. The perspective in the drawing opposite moves towards vanishing points up, down, left and right all at the same time.

No perspective line is truly straight. For most drawings though, the curvature is so slight as to be more or less invisible.

There's a cheat sheet at the back of the book to help you try out four point perspective ideas. It's really nothing more than lines drawn on a sphere – and this is what perspective is. Try it with some simple shapes first, building up to more complicated objects later.

Oh, yeah, here's that drawing opposite.

NOW FOR SOMETHING REALLY COMPLEX...

We're going to draw a cityscape from the top of a skyscraper.

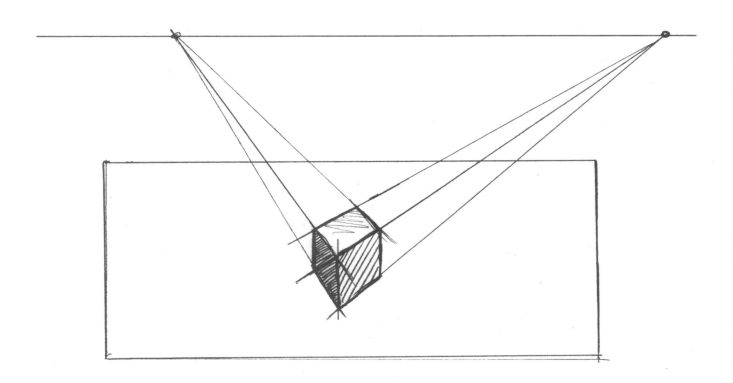

Step 1: Decide where to put the horizon line. In this case I'm going to be extra mean and put it above the top edge of the drawing!
What?! That's not fair!

Don't panic. As above, use a larger sheet of paper than the image you intend to draw.

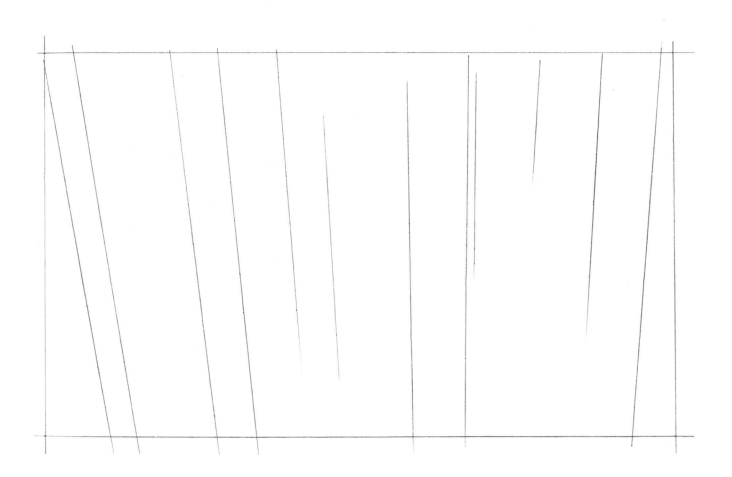

Step 2: Establish your vertical perspective. To help you out, I've included a 'cheat sheet' on page 191 for this very purpose. Just make a copy and put it under your paper.

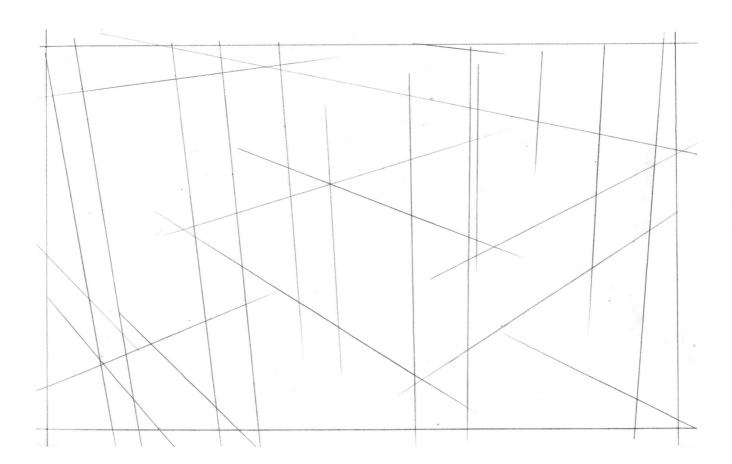

Step 3: Draw some two point horizontal perspective lines as above. Avoid grouping them too closely. Don't worry about their actual position at this stage, it's not important, as you're about to find out.

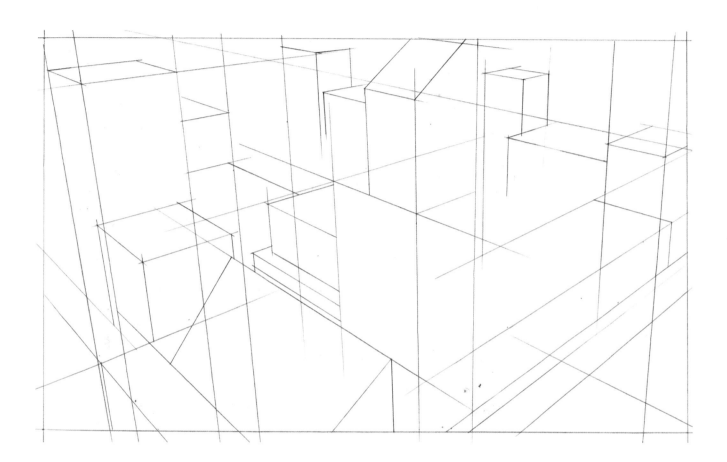

Step 4: This is where the fun starts. Use your imagination to 'suggest' possible locations for buildings. Some of the lines are already there, so let's make use of them. Fill in the missing parts of the major building's rooftops first.

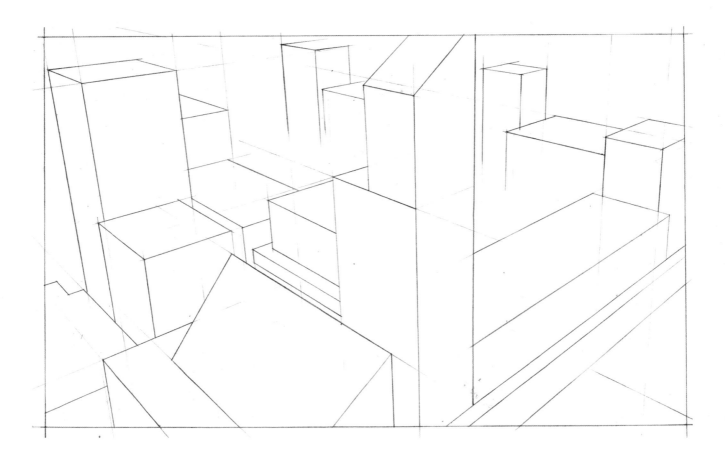

Step 5: Begin 'blocking in' the major buildings as above:
We're going to have as wide a variety of architecture as we like – old and new together
(hey – we may as well try things out)!

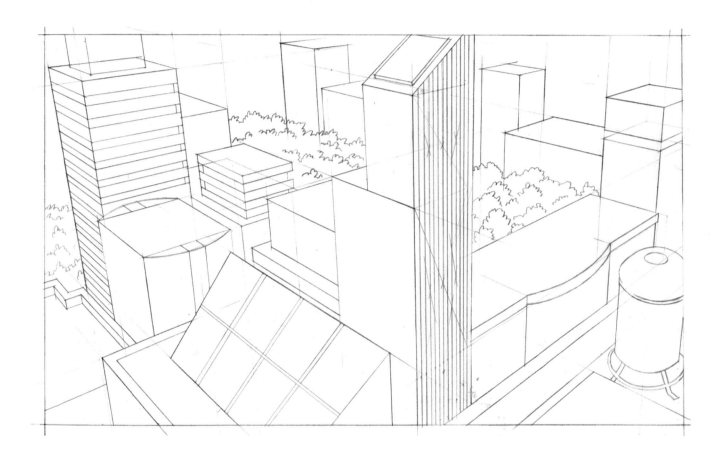

Step 6: Begin adding more detail to the foreground objects. Let's have some parkland in there, indicated by the trees.

151

Step 7: Add more detail. Remember that rooftops are hardly ever bare. Water towers, solar panels and air conditioning ducts are just some of the things you'll find perched on top of them.

Step 8: Let's finish that background. Like we did with the major buildings, put in a few perspective lines at random and let your imagination fill in the gaps. Any background buildings should be penciled very loosely and lightly. Don't fuss over detail.

Step 9: Tighten up any undefined areas and make any necessary last minute corrections. Make sure everything you need for inking is there – you don't want to be changing your mind when it's halfway inked.

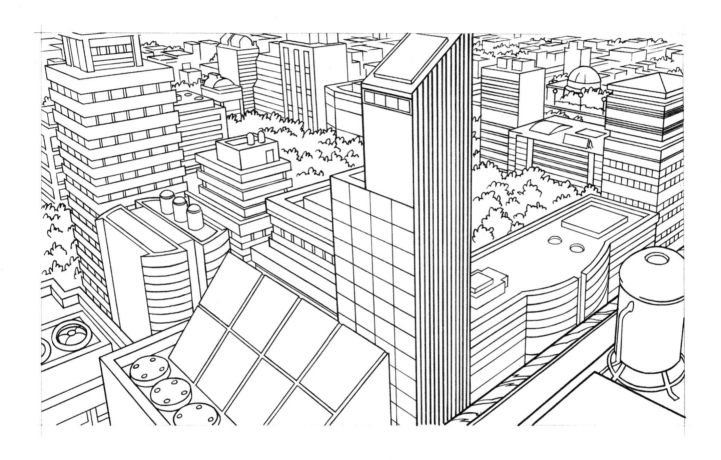

Step 10: Ink it! More detail on this follows in chapter 11.

CHAPTER 10

STORYTELLING AND
SPECIAL EFFECTS

STORYTELLING

Storytelling in the context of this book means putting together a series of images in such a way that the reader has as easy a reading experience as possible.

There are three key points to remember when beginning to tell any story:

1. Establish the location
You need to get the reader up-to-speed as quickly as possible. If they're asking themselves: "Where is all this taking place?", they're going to be distracted. A distracted reader is going to lose interest quickly.

2. Establish the characters
If the reader doesn't care about the characters you're using, the story will not engage them. The reader has to be able to relate to at least one of your characters – and as quickly as possible.

3. Ask a question
Most great stories begin with questions unanswered. The most obvious is: "Who killed them? And why?" Less obvious may include: "Why is this trainee vet so keen to avoid working with dogs?" Whatever your story, you have to get your reader hooked, so that they want to read on.

This is why the 'splash' page was invented. The first page of your story has the job of doing all three of the above. The first panel of your story splash page will normally occupy most of, if not all of the page. On this page you must, at the very least, give your reader some flavor of the above three points.

Have a good look at the following pages, which illustrate the three elements above.

EXAMPLE OF A 'SPLASH' PAGE

PANEL 1 DETAIL

What have we worked out from the visuals that the dialogue didn't tell us?

In panel 1 the gun in shot is still smoking, as are the bodies. We don't need to be told what's happened – we've established that purely through the image.

The location is a devastated urban landscape, seemingly completely abandoned.

The two dead and the two hiding behind the wrecked car are obviously related in some way – they all wear the same insignia. This is made important by a casual but prominent placement in panel 2 (see opposite page).

The pair hiding seem completely unarmed. Should they be discovered they would be at the mercy of the assassins.

Through a combination of dialogue and visuals we've satisfied the three criteria and created suspense. What happens in the next panel? Will they be discovered? Will the assassins pay for murdering the two dead?

PANEL 2 AND 3 DETAIL

KNOW WHERE YOU'RE GOING

Once you have the ending for your story it's really just a case of getting from A to C. This part, B, can involve sub-plots, flashbacks and other devices. The main thing to remember is that you are taking your reader on a journey.

GET THE BALANCE RIGHT

Too much information can be as bad as not enough. Two whole pages of head shots and dialogue is almost always a bad idea. But so is six pages of battle scenes that do little to advance the story. At the other end of the scale, three different locations/scenes on one page are likely to be stretching your reader's attention span to its snapping point.

SHOW, DON'T TELL

Being heavy-handed and clubbing the reader over the head with your ideas will result in them feeling either patronized or just plain cheated. Always give your reader an even chance of working stuff out for themselves. After all, this is what makes reading a rewarding experience.

DIALOGUE BALLOONS

Also known as speech bubbles, these come in many shapes and sizes, a selection of which are pictured above. Whether you hand-letter or use a computer to produce your dialogue, always remember to plan ahead and leave sufficient space in your artwork for your balloons. It's a good idea to roughly indicate on your artwork the size and position of your dialogue balloons.

SPECIAL EFFECTS AND OTHER DEVICES

What would manga be without speed lines, explosions and onomatopoeia (words that imitate sound)? There are a few manga titles which hardly use any of the above but the vast majority rely heavily on these effects for their dynamism.

SPEED LINES
High-speed car chases or sudden expressions of emotion are typical uses of speed lines. Some manga strips feature such excessive use of speed lines you'd think the artist hated drawing backgrounds.

They are simple enough to create but a few guidelines will be helpful:

Don't start your lines all at the same point. If you look at the image below you'll notice our lines have 'ragged' start points. This helps to create a feeling of energy. When surrounding an object, this jaggedness gives off the feeling of an 'energy glow'.

Don't make all your lines the same width. For much the same reasons as the previous tip, having lines all the same gauge will make your speed lines look lifeless and dull.

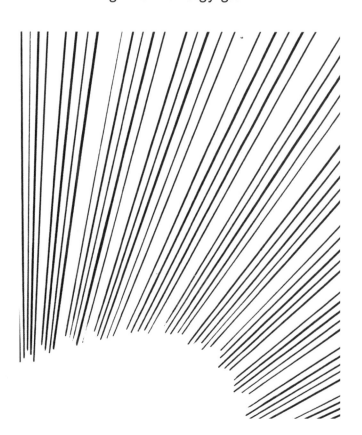

UP IN SMOKE

Smoke, clouds and other visible gases all have structure, just like solid objects. The key to drawing good smoke is capturing something of the way it moves and behaves.

The above method of drawing smoke is both simple and effective. The plumes twist as the smoke rises upwards and billows out. This is quite a large smoke cloud – smaller clouds would be more 'wispy' and billow less.

OUT WITH A BANG

Let's combine our speed lines and smoke to create an awesome explosion.

We'll also make use of some onomatapoeia – that's the 'whoom' sound and add some flying debris for good measure.

When stuff blows up it never does so in one uniform direction. Notice that the smoke cloud is not symmetrical and is 'lumpy'.

Cross-hatching can be very effective for darkening the heart of our explosions. Just remember to think through what parts of the cloud the light source will illuminate.

CHAPTER 11

INKS

AN INKLING OF INKING

A manga drawing generally isn't ready for print until those gray pencil lines have been converted to solid blacks. It's often a problem for the novice artist to make the step from pencilled art to finished inks. Why? Let's look at some of the potential pitfalls.

Confidence
This is the biggest barrier to good, finished artwork. The fear of messing things up at the final hurdle, just when you've got the pencils looking great, can be very strong.

My pencils look great as they are, thank you!
Remember this: you only did the pencils in the first place in order to produce finished, inked artwork. Pencilled artwork in manga is rarely an end in itself.

Getting hung up on detail: where to start and when to finish?
When is an inked page inked enough? If you don't know when to stop, chances are you didn't plan ahead enough. There's always a temptation to start inking before the image is actually ready to be inked. Don't give in to temptation. Make sure every pencil line represents what you ultimately want to ink.

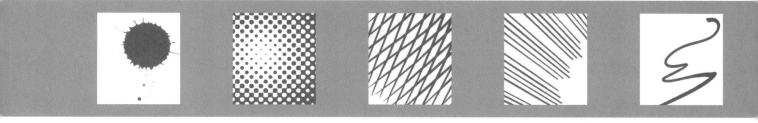

LET'S GET IT ALL WRONG

The above pencils are ready for inking. Every element is in place and the lines and shading are well-defined. However, in inexperienced hands the strength and dynamism of the panel can be totally wrecked.

On the next page is the worst possible inked version of the above. I've tried to include every inking mistake under the sun.

See how many glaring errors you can see. Every inch of the image has something fundamentally wrong with it.

Could it be worse? Probably. But at least it's potentially instructive.

Compare the above with the previous page and try to identify as many different inking errors as possible.

The two biggest problems with the inks here are indecision and lack of cohesion. The image completely fails to hang together as a credible picture. It looks like the job was started before key decisions were made – nearly always a fatal error.

This ink job is so very, very bad that I could spend all day describing its horrors. Fortunately for you, I only have a few pages to play with.

We'll go through them one by one starting with the main human characters.

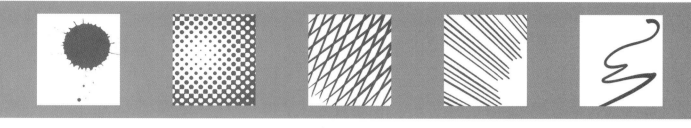

Error 1:

On the male figure's face the actual drawing has been seriously interfered with. An attempt to add detail to an already perfectly functional face has ended in the confused and horrible features you see opposite.

Error 2:

Either side of the character's chin are some nasty smudge marks. This has happened either because of impatience or just plain carelessness. Never work near an area where you may suspect the ink has not properly dried.

Error 3:

An attempt has been made to ink the hair as if it were individual strands, ruining the solid, chunky black field in the original pencils. The penciler didn't intend this – the highlights should be surrounded by solid black.

Error 4:

The character is in the foreground, but he's been inked with the kind of weak, skinny line you'd usually use for a background object. Similarly, the girl behind him, although inked fairly competently has been inked much too heavily.

Error 5:

The background is ridiculously confused. The high contrast takes the attention away from the action, focusing on an unimportant area. The cross-hatching is ugly and inappropriate and the mix of styles is an affront to the eyes.

Error 6:
What should be a menacing, hugely strong cyborg brute has been rendered in a weak, fussy style. His figure is now so poorly defined, only his head really tells us what he is. This style of inking would be better suited to smoke, shadow or some other more mysterious entity.

Error 7:
The long blast from the gun should start with a thick line and then taper as it reaches its target. It's been inked the other way around adding to the visual confusion.

Error 8:
The number '14' on the wall has been made solid black. As in error 5, this distracts. It looks pretty stupid too.

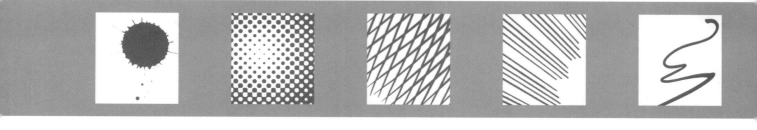

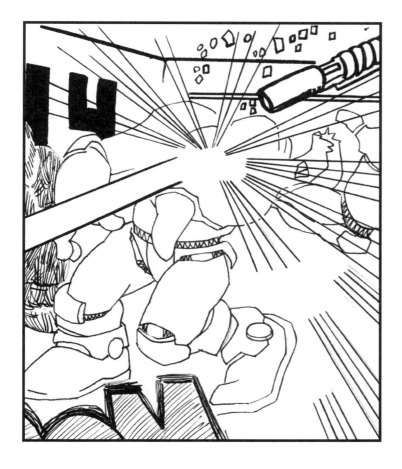

Error 9:
The grille and the ducts (in the image on the opposite page) have both suffered from the inker making mistakes which they have then attempted to 'patch over' with more lines and superfluous detail. This is a dumb idea and never works. Damage limitation earlier on, with the help of some whiteout would have been a better idea.

Error 10:
The second cyborg has been inked quite competently, but way too thinly. This makes him look ghost-like and insubstantial. The line also lacks any real expression. Basically the inker has merely traced over the pencils with just about zero creative input of his own. This is typically a mark of underconfidence. This inker must learn to be bolder and to bring some amount of personal style to his work.

Error 11:
The particles exploding off the cyborg's body have been inked far too uniformly. They don't seem to be moving, just strangely hanging in mid-air.

Error 12:
Both the back wall and the cyborg's gun have been inked far too heavily. The reader is left clueless as to the distance of almost all the elements in the panel. This section in particular is almost totally lacking in any visual clues, leaving the viewer baffled as to what exactly is before them.

Error 13
Both this gun and the male character's weapon have been inked in a variety of styles, all of which are pretty lousy. It's nearly always a bad idea to mix, say, pointilism, cross-hatching and regular line work. The inker should have made his mind up on which style to use before starting, and then stuck to it. This is a typical example of a lack of proper planning causing a problem which has then been made even worse by aimless doodling. Any experimenting should only be done at the pencil stage.

Error 14:
Sound effects like this one are meant to be loud. They should usually be the boldest thing on the page, yet this inker has attemped some silly cross-hatching, damping down the impact of the sound.

LET'S GET IT ALL RIGHT

The above image is much more like it. Attention is focused on the action and away from the incidental parts of the image. Elements in the foreground 'feel' closer to the viewer. The background serves its purpose and nothing more. There is little or no unnecessary detail. Lines are confidently rendered and appropriate for the depth of field.

What is depth of field?
The nearer to the horizon objects are, the less well-defined they appear to be. Objects in the foreground should be rendered boldly – with detail and strongly defined lines. Foreground objects should contain more and larger areas of pure black ink. The further an object recedes from the viewer the more you should lower both the contrast and the definition. Putting a huge amount of detail into objects near the horizon line is just a waste of time and will only complicate your image. Remember – everything fades to gray the closer it is to the horizon.

HOW TO MAKE DEPTH OF FIELD WORK

Foreground: Strong, bold lines, heavy blacks and more detail.

Midground: A little less detail, smaller areas of black and less contrast generally.

Background: Very little contrast – everything should be shades of gray. Low on detail. Think about where you are trying to focus the readers' attention. Heavy blacks will always draw attention. Try to use them to lure the reader in to the most important part of the image.

HOW TO HOLD A BRUSH/PEN

This technique is similar to the one used for pencilling. When inking from point A to point B you should not look at what you are inking. This may sound strange at first, but it's absolutely true. You should always look at where you're inking *to* – not where your brush or pen is inking *now*. You have to learn to trust your hand to do the job you've asked it to do. This will result in a constant, steady line.

LOW-FRICTION HANDS

Any part of your hand that comes into contact with the paper will cause friction while you ink. This friction affects your ability to make a clean line. It's therefore really important to have clean hands: dirty hands make bumpy, uneven lines.

HOW MUCH INK?

If you try to ink a page with insufficient ink on your brush or pen the following will happen: Halfway through inking a long line, your pen or brush will run dry. You'll then have to pick the line up halfway, which is not easy.

Your blacks will quickly turn gray once you erase the pencil lines. This can give you problems when it comes to reproduction. Your art won't look as nice, either. You should try to use as full a brush/pen as you're comfortable with. That way you'll get a nice, hard line that will survive erasing.

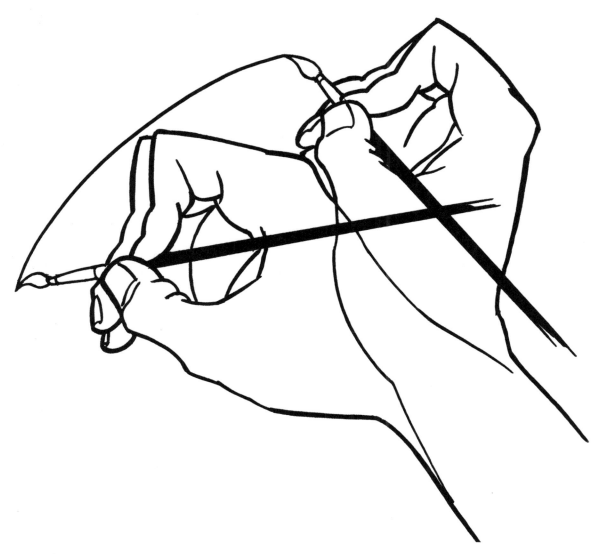

USE THE NATURAL ARC OF YOUR HAND

As explained earlier, the best way to draw a curved line is to position your hand so that it uses the natural 'flow' of your wrist to do the work. Get the artwork at the right angle to exploit the natural mechanics of your hand and you should be able to get it right every time.

Tone sheets are made of clear plastic with an adhesive backing. They're used to apply areas of gray to an image in a form which is easily reproduced, even on the cheapest quality paper. Of course they're not actually gray at all but are made up of tiny black dots, distributed at smaller or greater intervals, depending on the shade of gray required.

They come in many grades, both in dot size and spacing. The right dot size for your image depends partly on personal preference but also on your print requirements. If your page is going to appear in print smaller than the original artwork then you don't want too small a dot size. At a certain point, reprographic equipment will be unable to tell the dot from the space around it and the whole area will be reduced to black. If in doubt, go with a larger grade.

Here's how you apply them:

Cut a piece of the sheet slightly larger than the area you're working on. Apply it to the artwork, making sure it overlaps the outline. Use a sharp blade such as a scalpel to trim the tone sheet. Work in the middle of the black outline to give yourself some margin for error. Peel off the excess – you're done.

TONED AND READY

Pencilled, inked, toned and ready for press. And at least a little more beautiful than our mystery inker's efforts.

It can take many years of practice to get really confident with our ink line. Over the course of time we get comfortable with our own style as we learn new tricks and techniques.

But the biggest leap we can make is when we've inked so many pages that we can look at the pencils and know almost to the line how it's going to come out. Ultimately our inking style is like our handwriting and should not reflect self-consciousness.

CHAPTER 12

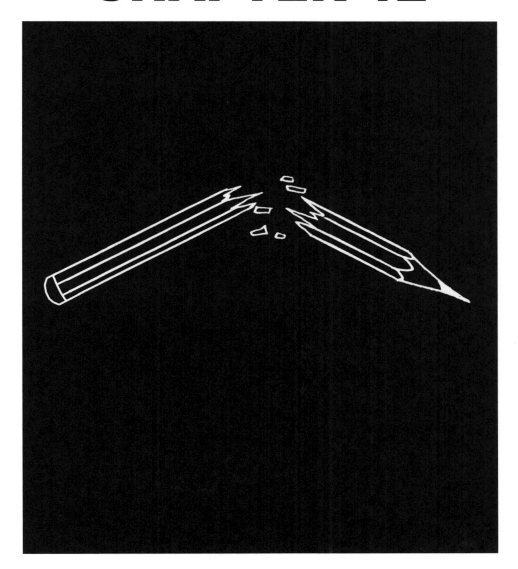

HINTS AND TIPS

GOOD TO KNOW

This final chapter is about tidying up loose ends and providing some useful advice. Turn to it when you get stuck or just feel like some new ideas.

Everyone gets stumped sooner or later. This chapter will at least provide you with some possible solutions.

The cheat sheets on the final two pages will help in drawing images of the kind found in chapter 9.

Good luck.

DRAW EVERY DAY

This is simply the most important thing you can do to improve your drawing. The learning process can be mysterious at the best of times but if we follow this simple rule something very important will happen. Our brains will become permanently set up to think visually. Our minds will be far better placed to draw on all the visual information we've soaked up. As a result, once-difficult problems become easy.

Keeping inspirational material around is a good idea. When we look at the work of great artists this can often give us the jolt we need to grab pencil and paper.

PLAN AHEAD

When a page goes horribly wrong or simply doesn't turn out as planned it's usually because of bad planning. For instance, it's just plain silly to embark upon a 200-page cyberpunk epic without doing, at the very least, a breakdown of the key stages of development.

CREATIVE BLOCKS

These come in many different forms and are generally more frustrating than any other kind of problem. Stuck for an idea? Can't think of an ending? Can't think of a beginning? If you've been banging your head against the proverbial wall for hours and have still come up with nothing, you have two real options available to you.

First option: put it to compost. This means put it to one side and forget about it. Sleep on it. Your brain needs some fresh input before it can come up with something inspired.

Second option: approach the problem in a completely different way. Do not allow yourself to go anywhere near the now-stale ideas you've been kicking around. Do something entirely random, no matter how stupid it seems. You need to make a leap into the unknown in order to generate some new ideas.

USING THUMBNAILS

A thumbnail is a smaller, quicker version of what we finally want to do. The clearer the idea is in your head, the easier it will be to achieve your aims. It's often a big leap from an idea sitting abstractly in our imaginations to the finished artwork on the page, so any tools at our disposal to bridge the gap should be used.

You may recognize the image above from chapter 2. It's an initial idea sketch of the Android factory. Most of the visual information is already present, though it's lacking a lot of detail. The point of it is to establish the basic setting and characters.

Thumbnail drawings can be either barely recognizable squiggles to help us see the layout and placement of speech balloons or they can be almost fully rendered preliminary versions or studies of the final work. Whichever it is, they are there to help us organize our thoughts and deal with potential problems before they happen.

USING COMPUTERS AND PREPARING FOR PRINT

As mentioned in chapter 1, computers can be an invaluable tool for finishing artwork. They are no substitute for drawing skills though, no matter how powerful and clever our machines may become.

Using a good graphics program we can clean up ink spills, add tone or color and increase contrast, as well as format our image for print. They are also great for adding speech bubbles and text as we are free to adjust and modify the size of our balloons and text until they complement the artwork. However, you should keep all your text sizes consistent. A sudden drop or increase in text size from panel to panel looks bad and is an unwanted distraction.

A good quality scanner is an invaluable tool for getting our images into the computer. Remember that when scanning your artwork, it should be scanned at at least 300 dpi (dots per inch). This is the minimum quality necessary for print. It may look fine on the screen at 72 dpi but when printed will either be tiny or look horribly fuzzy. For best results, scan your images at between 350 and 600 dpi – you can always reduce the quality later – but you can never increase the quality once you've committed.

There are various standard image formats for print. It's a good idea to check with the person ultimately printing your artwork which format is right for them. If in doubt, TIFF is a good format – it's very high quality and importantly can be handled by both PC and Macintosh machines.

Another useful device is a printer. These have become cheaper and cheaper while all the time becoming better quality. If you are printing your manga yourself, you should give some consideration to the paper you print on. It makes a massive difference to the final quality of your images.

CHEAT SHEETS

You may remember me mentioning these in the perspective chapter. They are invaluable tools for making difficult perspective easier. They are meant to be placed under your artwork as guides. Space restrictions of this book mean they cannot be very big, but if you need bigger versions, simply blow them up on a photocopier. Alternatively, if you have access to a computer with a graphics program you can make up your own by following the principles in chapter 9.

WHAT SEPARATES SO-SO MANGA FROM GREAT MANGA?

This is a subject that needs a whole book dedicated to it. It's usually easier to criticize bad manga, than it is to explain exactly what makes a great piece of artwork. So let's first look at where we can go wrong.

HACK WORK

We can nearly always tell when artwork has been churned out with little or no interest in trying to achieve anything beyond paying the bills. Shoddy anatomy, sloppy finishing, sub-standard backgrounds are less than professional. At the other end of the scale there are artists who would rather starve than turn in anything less than a masterpiece. These are people who often blow deadlines and give their editors' nightmares. Getting a balance between these two extremes will allow you to maintain your sanity and keep you in work.

THE DEFINITION OF PROFESSIONALISM

Professionalism is simply this: doing the best job possible in the time you have. That means if you only have two weeks to do a job that would normally take you three, you'd better figure out a way to cut some corners without sacrificing the artistry. Sound tough? Well it is. The world of manga requires some serious output – it isn't for the faint-hearted!

At the same time, drawing for a living is one of the most rewarding occupations imaginable. Of all the hundreds of artists I have met, I am yet to meet one who would swap their job for anyone else's.

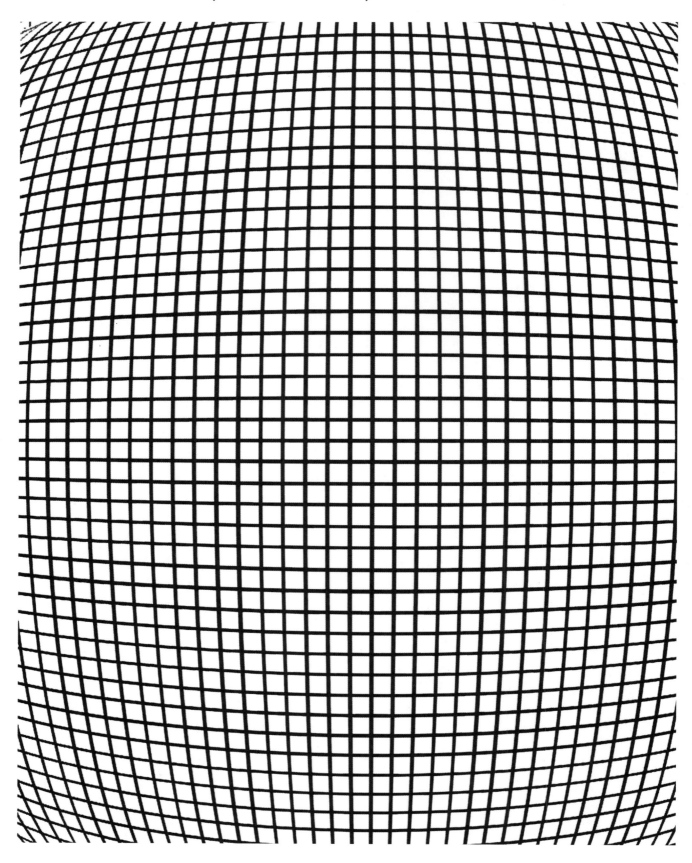

CHEAT SHEET 2 (SEE PAGE 147)